CRUSHED
FOR
FRAGRANCE

A REAL LIFE STORY

MARGARET NEWNES

PRESS

Crushed for Fragrance
A Real Life Story
by Margaret Newnes

Printed in the United States of America

ISBN- 978-1-60477-435-1

First print 1992
Second edition 1996
Third edition 2001

www.xulonpress.com

FOREWORD

There is something about Margaret Newnes that makes you want what she has got. She is warm, friendly, gentle and vivacious; her infectious laugh... the mischievous twinkle in her eye... her lovable disposition...make her one of the most winsome persons you will ever meet. Not that she is a saint (once you meet her you will be glad for the fact that she is not) for the very thing that makes her life so strikingly attractive is her warm-blooded humanness. Margaret Newnes is an ordinary woman and delightfully content to be just so! But her zest for life, love for her family, and her passionate devotion to truth and to God blend together in a deeply moving life-story, powerful in its simplicity and candour.

"CRUSHED FOR FRAGRANCE" is about life as it is...about family... school… faith... dream...love... humor.... . But most of all about what C.S.Lewis calls 'God's mega phone'…PAIN! It is the story of a courageous woman's struggle to cope with the painful contradictions of life. What is the source of her fortitude when tragedy strikes so suddenly and cruelly?

How does she display such remarkable strength in the face of trauma and adversity? You will have to read this book to discover Margaret Newnes' answers to these crucial questions. Her answers have a burning and convincing authenticity that more sophisticated philosophical deliberations do not possess simply because she speaks as one who has experienced the fiery furnace at maximum heat.

Strange as it might seem, however, this is not a depressing book, for through the dark clouds of tragedy, sorrow and conflict in her pilgrimage through life, shines the unmistakable radiance of a wholesome and vibrant faith that will refresh and challenge the heart of every reader.

That is indeed the beautiful fragrance of Margaret Newnes' life that touches us through this book. That this fragrance should reach you, the reader, and enable you to encounter the source of the author's comfort and strength in the face of life's painful trials is, I believe, the sincere desire of the author, and the intention with which this book has been written.

(Dr.) Rev. Ivan Morris Satyavrata
Senior Pastor And Chairman of
Assemblies of God Mission,
Calcutta...India

Dear Reader,

*E*ver thought you would hold a miracle in your hands?

Well, your moment has finally arrived. This book you are now holding is more than just a story about a God who can perform miracles. The book is a miracle in itself!

If it were not for Jesus, you would have neither the story nor the book. His amazing grace, His power and His abundant provision, mark the story you are about to read. As well as the story that is behind the writing, printing and publishing of this testimony.

So it is to Him that I owe my highest, deepest and most sincere gratitude and thanks.

You will discover that this is a book about a family and friends; as well as a book by family and friends. Without their help, the manuscripts would not have been written, improved, edited, typed and printed.

More importantly, they provided all the encouragement and the will I needed to faithfully carry out the Lord's command since I started writing this book way back in…Yes…1984!

Space and time will not allow me to mention all their names. My deepest thanks to each of them in India and abroad that made this book possible.

They have helped put this story in your hands, so that the fragrance of Jesus may live in your heart.

To Him be glory and praise!

Yours in Christ,
Margaret Newnes

A few extracts from letters from readers of "Crushed For Fragrance"

A splendid effort. What a moving recital of exceptional courage, faith and fortitude. It should be a source of inspiration and comfort to countless readers who should be encouraged to raise the level of the threshold of personal pain. The spirit of evangelism is overpowering. Perhaps one day, it will demand full time consideration.

When my friend read your book, she was so impressed. It made quite an impact on her. She contacted the publishers and ordered 50 copies to distribute amongst her friends. Your testimony is spreading like wild fire and having a good and powerful impact on peoples' lives.

At every step of your wonderful book, one is guided and deep faith forms, in leading you to the simple formulas of life -- love, truth and faith. The satisfaction derived from reading your book was tremendous. You will be surprised; I am a Hindu, looking for the common factors, which bind humanity — much above caste, class and religion.

The author's style is rich in simplicity. Her sound reasoning and fast pace of unfolding her life story make the book easy to read. The title "Crushed for Fragrance" is irreplaceable. The title is original, so meaningful and peculiar.

In the course of reading the book, every skeptic gets convinced in the tangible love of the living God.

I got so absorbed in your book. It was a most enriching experience. May your life and example be an inspiration to many more.... Could not put it down.

What a marvelous record of the goodness of the Lord to you and your family over the years. I am sure you will continue to experience His faithfulness in the days ahead.

The autobiography is appealing due to the author's sincerity, faith, beautiful personality and determination. She is a life warrior who overcomes all difficulties. The author has always been in inspiring rapport with her Provider, Comforter and most intimate Friend.

CHAPTER 1

D r. Leggett was not aware of it, nor was his wife, Marjorie. But what they had so lovingly planned for during the preceding nine months was about to be the surprise of their lives. Everyone was expecting Michael.

The Leggett's British Army hospital quarters at Kamptee, Central India, was bursting with anticipation. The eldest child June, who was three years old, and her brother Noel, who was nearly two, would go daily to their mother's bed, peeping on tiptoe, enquiring if Michael had arrived.

Why Michael? Well, how could it be anyone else? Joseph and Marjorie's third baby was due on 29th September, the feast of St. Michael. So, Michael it had to be. There was no doubting that.

Even the fact that Mum was asked to sleep in at the hospital a few nights prior to the baby's arrival did not shake their faith. Michael was sure to arrive on schedule.

Then, on 27th September 1937 at seventeen minutes past three in the afternoon, the unexpected happened. I was born. Margaret Rose!

While the family rejoiced and laughed over me, they anguished over Mum. She suffered quite a bit at my birth, and could have lost her sight completely. It was only several years later that I realized she was spared total blindness. I thanked God.

We were in Kamptee for nearly three years. It is only a name in my memory of what I was told of our family life there. I was too young to make memories of my own. The name Kamptee has been a part of my beginnings... but Bombay, a very large city on the west coast of India, where we went from Kamptee, began to form memories in me. We lived in Colaba Chambers in Bombay. I remember watching my 'Khaki Soldier Dad' go to work daily. I loved it when my 'Khaki Soldier' returned home. He would carry me on his shoulders and I would laugh, happy to be so high above everything.

Mum's eyesight had not improved since I was born. One day Dad brought a German doctor home for tea. As Mum entertained them, she gave each a cup of tea and also filled their saucers. The doctor watched her as she kept pouring and wondered. Dad was most apologetic and explained Mum's loss of vision. "What a pity," said the doctor, "if only she had come to Bombay earlier, we might have done something for her." I remember thinking later of what Bombay might have meant to my mother, if we had only been there earlier.

Bombay in the early '40s rang with loud ear-piercing air raid warnings. We would immediately turn off the lights and grope around in candlelight. We would then get under the table. As a child, this war exercise seemed an exciting game.

It was not long after this, that another change took place. War was declared. Dad had to leave and go to the Middle East. Our family was now only Mum, June, Noel and myself.

It meant more packing, more news of moving. Mum, with her failing eyesight, could not handle all three of us alone. So prospectuses of boarding schools were sent for, and before long, Noel and June were heading for a boarding school way down south in Yercaud. The school was situated in the Shevaroy Hills. I was just over four years old at the time and accompanied Mum as she took June and Noel to school.

The nuns welcomed us so warmly and fussed over me. They carried me about and showered me with sweets and kisses. They showed me the huge playing fields surrounded by trees laden with pears. It seemed like Paradise. The school buildings were so clean and well kept. I can still picture every part of that massive layout. When it was time for goodbyes, I also wished Mum goodbye and said I would stay in school with June and Noel. It was only later that it occurred to me that Mum had intended leaving me in school if I liked it.

Mum traveled home on her own.

My bed was near the nun who was in charge of the dormitory. At night she would come and tuck me into bed. I felt so loved and cared for that I did not feel homesick. As I grew older however, it got harder to leave home each year.

At that early and impressionable age of four, I followed all the religious practices and traditions in school. They became a part of my life. I observed children of seven and eight years being prepared for their First Holy Communion. By the time I was five, I was determined to make mine as well. I attended the Catechism classes with the older children. We were taught to be sorry for our sins and confess them to the priest, so that we could be ready to receive Jesus into our hearts. I did not really understand about sin, but I did want to wear my long white dress and veil and become a 'Bride of Christ.'

I was so excited. I could not wait for Jesus to come into my heart by receiving Him on my First Holy Communion Day. I was encouraged to write home to Mum and tell her how much I wanted to make my Communion and that I would cry if she did not allow me to do so. Being so young, someone had to write the letter for me, as I dictated it. Mum consented. I was bursting with joy as I went up with the other 'brides' to receive JESUS in my heart on my First Communion Day.

CHAPTER 2

World War II was over! And Dad was back. He had medals to show he had been in action and many tales to share with us. We would sit around and listen with awe and admiration, as he would relate in detail the narrow brushes he and his comrades had with death. "And there were we," he would start in his loud sonorous voice, "in our tents. We could hear the bombs whiz past. Many times we had just left a place and gone ahead and we would look back to see it go up in flames." Dad seemed a real hero to us and his stories never grew dull. Even though we heard him repeat these tales over and over, we would still sit and listen with great big eyes and greater interest.

Now Dad was home, but where was home for me? June, Noel and I were boarders at Yercaud. Dad was now posted at Barrackpore in West Bengal. Mum went with him there. June later left Yercaud due to ill health and was admitted into the Good Shepherd Convent in Bangalore. It was important for her to be near our aunts in Bangalore, who could look after her when necessary. Noel had graduated to Montfort, the boys' school. Now our family was divided, separated by thousands of miles. Mum and Dad in Barrackpore, June in Bangalore, Noel in Montfort - the boys' school in Yercaud - and I, in Sacred Heart Girls' School, Yercaud.

Not long after, I received a letter from Mum and Dad in Barrackpore announcing the news of an addition to our family. I was not the youngest any longer. I now had a younger sister Sybil. I was only nine years old then. Having led such a sheltered life in the Convent, I had no idea about the 'birds and the bees' and I wondered how my sister was born. I was so naive that when I was told she had been dropped from a plane, which flew over our house, I believed it!

Now that the holidays had begun, I looked forward to seeing my baby sister. I soon became a little mother to her. But all too soon the holidays had come to an end. Mum and Dad had decided that it was better for me to be with June in Good Shepherd Convent in Bangalore. As much as I loved my school in Yercaud and the nuns who so lovingly cared for me, I felt it was wiser to be with my sister.

The school in Bangalore was run by another order of nuns. They too had a great influence on me. I wanted to follow in their footsteps. But for now we had to follow Dad, who was posted to Mathura, not far from Agra. We were moving again. This time to a Convent run by the Jesus and Mary nuns, which was located just opposite the jail.

I will never forget alighting at the Agra bus station and asking the cycle rickshawallah to take us to the Convent. He could not understand us. We tried hard to explain and at last he said, "You mean 'chotta jail'?" Even among the locals it was referred to as the 'small jail.' As we approached the Convent with its high gray walls, we realized why it was known as the small jail. Where were we heading?

Traveling from the South to the North affected our education. The standard of Hindi was so advanced in the North; we found it really difficult to cope. I knew however, God would help me whenever I called upon Him.

God having answered my prayers on many occasions increased my faith in Him. This, coupled with the influence of the nuns whom I observed wherever I went, made me want to follow in their footsteps. In like manner, I would never be found without my bunch of medals and my scapular. I had what they called 'My Steps to Heaven' a whole pile of prayer books, which I would read daily. I would make Novenas and recite numerous prayers. Saying the Rosary daily was a **must**. Being a boarder, I attended Mass every morning in the school chapel. I belonged to the True Religion and felt sorry for those who did not belong to the same. Yet, in spite of that, there was a great emptiness and vacuum in my life, which I could not explain.

Two years later we were moving again. Dad was posted to Santa Cruz in Bombay. June and I were admitted into St. Joseph's Convent in Bandra. We could have been day scholars, but after living such sheltered lives all these years, Bombay really scared us. I could not cross the road myself. The buses and heavy traffic petrified me. For one year we were boarders and then as we got the feel of city life, we became day scholars. I just had a year of schooling left before my school days would be left behind me.

After completing my Senior Cambridge exam in Bandra, I took my Junior School and Kindergarten Teachers' Training at the Convent of Jesus and Mary Byculla, in Bombay. By some coincidence it was called St. Margaret's Training College.

Once again nuns surrounded me. But this time it was not their footsteps I would be following in. I was chasing fun and excitement with my new friends. In the first year of my training, I became the ringleader of much fun and mischief. When the lecturer was late for class, I would tell my classmates to open their desks. Then, I would count: "One, two, three..." And the lids would come down together. BANG! What a commotion and noise! In the twinkling of an eye, there would be such innocence on our faces as the lecturer walked in.

During the monsoons, I would encourage the girls who used to travel by local train with me, to stand under the overhead pipes from the rooftops so that we would get soaking wet. We would walk into college shivering, hoping to be offered a cup of hot cocoa. All we were told was to go and change and proceed to class straightaway, as we were late enough! Surely the nuns could see who the ringleader was.

Apparently, the nuns had recognized these leadership qualities but desired them to be put to better use. So the following year I was elected Head girl. I was given added responsibilities. I had to be in college on time to take the roll call before Assembly. I had to be a real example to the juniors and my colleagues. In my first year, I would change the hands of the clocks during the afternoon session so that the bell would ring earlier for us to go home. Now I had matured with the responsibility given to me. Things were peaceful for the lecturers and the nuns.

Training was soon over and it was time for us to apply for jobs in various schools. I did not apply to any school, because by now, with the continued help and encouragement of Mother Berchmans (Berky) my lecturer-nun, I was certain I had a vocation. I wanted to join the Jesus and Mary Novitiate at Boat Club Road Poona and become a nun. I wrote home to tell my parents my plans. It came as a shock to them. My sister June told me this when I phoned home a few days later. " The house is like a graveyard," she said. " Mum is not talking. She is so upset at the thought of you becoming a nun."

I did not think Mum would feel like this. I went home the next weekend to ask her what her objections were. Both of us looked at each other. Instead of speaking, the lump in my throat was getting bigger. At last, I plucked up courage to ask her what she thought of my decision.

Mum explained that I had lived such a sheltered life all these years as a boarder. She thought that for me to go out into the world, as a teacher would be good. She then said that if I still wanted to become a nun after six months I could do so. I thought that was fair and was willing to try it out, knowing full well that I would definitely be heading for the Novitiate at the end of that time. Nothing and nobody would distract me from my call to become a nun.

CHAPTER 3

W e were dashing home on a Friday evening in September 1956, laden with assignments for the weekend. Just as I was approaching the gate, I was summoned to Mother Superior's office. I wondered if I had done something wrong. It was on very rare occasions that we entered this room. Once I went in, however, I was at peace, as I saw the kindness in Mother Felix's eyes. She beckoned to me. "Sit down my child," she said. At once I relaxed. "Are you very disappointed that you cannot join the Novitiate in January?"

"Yes Mother. You know how very much I want to join the Convent."

"Anyway my child," she continued, "you must honor your parents' decision. Your mother wants you to go out into the world and teach for six months. I also think this will be good for you. In this way you can at least test your vocation."

"Yes Mother," I replied humbly. What else could I say? There was no alternative.

"By the way Margaret, have you thought of which school you would like to teach in?" asked Mother Superior.

"I hear there is a vacancy in Villa Theresa on Peddar Road Mother," I replied. "In fact, I was thinking of going there tomorrow to hand in my application personally."

Before I could leave the office, Rev. Mother held out a letter to me. " I have just received this letter from Father Schoch, Principal of the school attached to the National Defence Academy at Khadakwasla. He has asked me to send him three teachers. I immediately thought of you as one of them."

Khadakwasla? My heart leapt with excitement! Nine months earlier I had visited the N.D.A. with some friends. I was so impressed with the massive buildings, the cleanliness and orderliness. Everything seemed so posh. And now, I had been offered a job there! Should I jump at the offer? But what was Mother saying now? "Pray about it Margaret, and let me know by Monday if you agree. Father Schoch will come personally to interview the three teachers."

"Yes Mother, I shall pray about this and let you know on Monday. Thank you so much." As I rose from my seat, she patted me and said, "Go my child. God bless and guide you."

With a grateful heart I wished her and left her office. My step was lighter than when I had entered. While I waited at the bus stop at Clare Road, I toyed with this idea. Should I go to Khadakwasla or should I go for my interview to Villa Theresa the following day? I prayed about it. The double decker bus slowed down and I jumped in. All the way to Lower Parel, I kept praying. Getting through the crowds, entering the station, waiting for the local to take me to Santa Cruz, the same question went on churning in my mind: Villa Theresa or Khadakwasla?

Santa Cruz arrived all too soon and I had to merge with the crowds. I had to keep on pushing and being pushed as I climbed over the bridge and down to the bus stop. After a short halt in the queue, I caught the bus to Juhu Church. Having all this time to think and pray, I felt it would be a good idea to teach at the National Defence Academy.

The buzz in college on Monday was infectious! Groups of senior students were huddled together discussing their applications or reenacting their interviews. I pricked up my ears when I heard someone mention N.D.A. Khadakwasla. I turned round to find that Marcia and Audrey, my college mates planned to teach there. Evidently, Mother Superior had informed them of the vacancies.

Like me, Audrey too had wanted to become a nun. A few months earlier, she had been ill with thrombosis and had been home to Poona. While she was recuperating, a certain Air Force Officer named Douglas came into her life. He was stationed at the Air Force base at Lohegaon, Poona. Hardly anyone knew him as Douglas, but referred to this six-footer as Dinky!

When Audrey returned to college, she was a completely changed person. We would notice her beaming every alternate day. Faithful Dinky wrote to her regularly. She was in her element with each letter she received from him. Gone was Audrey's vocation. It was obvious that her days of wanting to become a nun were over and done with.

At the end of the week, we were informed that Father Schoch had come to interview his new teachers. He painted a glorious picture to each one of us in turn. We could not wait to go and teach in Khadakwasla. The salary was Rs.115/- per month! Half of it would go towards our board. What excitement!

He informed us that he would meet us at Poona Station on the 2nd of January 1957. It did seem too soon after the Christmas and New Year celebrations. All the same, we got ready to leave.

It was now time to bid farewell to all at home. Marcia and I met at Victoria Terminus Station, better known as V.T. We left by the 3.10 train on the 2nd afternoon. We chatted all the way and made friends with the other passengers. All too soon we reached Poona and spotted the familiar figure of Father Schoch. He had brought all the Poona-based teachers to welcome us. Dinky had brought Audrey to the station, so that we could all go together in Father's bus.

The teachers were very friendly and tried their best to converse with us. But nothing could stop me from feeling homesick. I did not like the idea of rushing off to work soon after New Year's Day. Surely we could have reopened a little later! We had hardly got over Christmas and here we were away from home, about to start our first job. The lump in my throat got bigger and bigger. And as we drove out of Poona Railway Station with this group of friendly teachers, I suddenly began to feel cold and lonely and afraid.

Would I be able to cope? What would these months hold for me? Questions went over in my mind and then suddenly, WOW! I was taken aback as the driver stopped by the side of the road. I could not believe my eyes. It was like fairyland, with big lights and small, twinkling in the valley below. The beauty of the lights shining in the darkness of the valley; how the sight of it lifted my questioning soul from the valley of despair.

Our bus took us past Ghol Market, then up the President's Driveway. I leaned against the cold, misty window to get a better view. Everything was so clean and spick and span. The squadrons lay on either side. Everywhere I looked, I saw neat rows of trees and flowers. It was delightful driving past all these impressive buildings. There was the imposing Administrative Block on the right, flanked by the Library and Theatre.The Parade Ground was to the left and a little further right was the Officers' Mess and swimming pool. I recognized it immediately. I was brought on a visit to this place just last year.

Seeing all the cleanliness and grandeur thus far, I could not wait to see our quarters. As we drove on, my mind formed its own pictures. I imagined a very modern looking cottage, neat and homely. "Almost there," called one of the teachers. The bus skirted a corner; we went right, then left, then straight ahead. "Home at last," they squealed in delight!

The three of us from St. Margaret's looked at each other and then at the place they called HOME! Was

this the place where we were going to stay? Perhaps this was the back entrance? No it was not! The others alighted from the bus in such excitement. They took out their luggage and went to their respective rooms. We were shown our room. We could not get over how old and dilapidated the building was. What a contrast to the splendor of the rest of the Academy. It seemed unbelievable. We did not know whether to laugh or cry. So we ended up doing both. What a homecoming!!

I would have run back home immediately if I could. The quarters were so decrepit that in the first few months, we moved twice, for safety reasons. In fact, the previous quarters were so old, they had to be demolished! So you can imagine their state and our shock when we first arrived. Once we got accustomed to the place, it did not matter where we stayed. In fact, we grew to like it, as the other teachers did. It became home to us also!

The scenery was breath taking. We had a wonderful view from our verandah. The road below our quarters skirted a placid lake with the dam across it. Each side we turned, we were surrounded by hills. We truly had a room with a view! The mornings were particularly beautiful. I will never forget the first day we stepped out of our room to the most spectacular sight. Dressed in rich cloaks of green, the hills sloped away from us on every side, and their peaks blazed with a golden brilliance as the morning sun shone on them. The air was fresh and the sky was clear.

A short while later, the principal's voice tore our minds away from the rapture of nature to the nature of our jobs. I drew a deep, nervous breath of Khadakwasla air, as he turned to read my responsibilities out to me.

I was in charge of the Nursery class. There were sixty-four children in my care. Only a handful could speak English. It was quite a challenge having such a class. I was raw...fresh from College. It was tough and tiring. But with God's help I managed to get across to the children. Fortunately, there was a piano for me to play in the class. This was a great asset. The class should have been divided into at least three divisions, but I had to manage on my own. Each child was given individual attention. I spent much time in preparing their books daily.

It was rewarding to see from scribbles and squiggles how these little children could learn to write so neatly. I loved all those children in my class. Each one was extremely special to me.

One day, as I was walking back from school, I prayed, "Lord, you know how much I love children. When I become a nun, there will be many more children to love... **but** they will not be my own children. So...if I find someone I really love and who loves me... I would like him to be the father of my children." Sshhhh! What a strange thought for one testing her vocation!! But there it was!! I tried to erase the thought from my mind, but it did not leave. The all-seeing and all-knowing God who even knows our thoughts before we think them... must have been having a little chuckle up there as He knew His plans ahead for me! I wondered. "Will it ever be?"

After coming to Khadakwasla, it suddenly dawned on me that this place had offered me the greatest gift of all –'freedom.' Having been brought up as a boarder in a convent all my life; I never enjoyed so much freedom. Even in Training College, I could not leave the premises without Mother's consent. So, once we settled in Khadakwasla and wanted to go out to town, we went to ask Father permission. The teachers who told us it was not necessary stopped us. I felt so strange to go out without asking permission. This was quite a contrast to the way I was brought up in boarding school and college.

Most of the teachers were from Poona or had relatives there. Every weekend they would dash away to get the bus for Poona. They would go home and return laden with tuck for the following week. Fortunately, because of my very good friend Dorothy from college, I became friendly with her family who lived in a lovely cottage on Kahun Road.

The Alphonsos made me feel very welcome and so I also had a home to go for weekends. We would take the afternoon bus to town. Our journey back was made in comfort and style. Audrey and Dinky would collect Marcia and me and drive us back in Dinky's black Ambassador. This was a weekly procedure and we enjoyed these drives.

On the last Sunday of January 1957, I had just packed my bag and was getting ready to leave, when I heard the familiar sound of Dinky's car. I gathered my belongings and went to thank the Alphonsos and wish them, when Dinky walked in looking very serious. I wondered if anything was wrong. Before I could ask, he put his arm around me and led me to a corner of the room. "I hope you don't mind Margaret, but I will not be driving you back tonight."

"Oh goodness," said I, "how do I get a bus to return at this hour of the night? Why didn't you inform me earlier?"

"No no," he replied, "you can come in my car, but I will not be driving. I am too tired. So I will sit behind with Audrey and relax. I hope you don't mind sitting in front with the Air Force driver." Beggars can't be choosers! I could not afford to be snooty! I did not mind sitting near any driver for that matter, as long as I got back to my quarters.

I gave the driver a casual glance as we approached the car. I was struck by how well he had turned out. He wore an immaculate white shirt and trousers, black socks and shiny shoes. He saluted smartly and opened the door for me to enter. Did I feel important! Even so, I got in most cautiously, pulled my dress over my knees as was customary for me to do, and sat as close to the door as possible.

I could feel the driver's eyes on me from time to time. Each time I would freeze. Every so often, he would apologize that the door was not secure enough and politely stretch across to close it securely. Each time he did this, I would get even closer to the door. If it was possible, I might have gone through the door! As this drama was being enacted in the front, I could hear loud kissing sounds and giggles from the back. I did not know where to turn. I dared not look right, towards the driver. I dared not turn back and see those two lovebirds. All I could do was keep my eyes fixed ahead and pray we would reach the N.D.A. as soon as possible.

After some time, Dinky was over-acting his role quite a bit. I came to the conclusion who the driver was. I became wise to what was going on and blurted out, "I know this fellow is PERCY." It was a name Dinky had often mentioned, but I had never met the person. The game was over and Dinky introduced me to Percy formally. How we all laughed! Percy and Dinky were roommates. In fact, they had joined the Air Force together. Later they were together at Agra, and now, they were posted in Poona, a quiet little city south of Bombay. They were quite a pair those two! I could not get over this trick they had planned. What a laugh we had! What an introduction!

Later I learned that Percy had just returned from leave and Dinky had spoken to him about me. He said, "Percy, there is a real nice girl I would like you to meet. She is Audrey's roommate. Come on, I will introduce you to her." And Percy replied, "Thanks so much Dinky. I have had enough of girls. I do not want to meet any more. From now on, I am going to concentrate on my trumpet and weight lifting." All the same, Dinky managed to pull him along that memorable night to drive us to the N.D.A. (God's ways are much higher...)

We drove from the Alphonsos' house to Jangli Maharaj Road in the city where we had to collect Marcia. Percy was from Bandra and so was Marcia, so extra precautions had to be taken. He disguised himself by tying a bright handkerchief round his head and put on a pair of goggles. What a scream he looked! We were hysterical. I sat at the back with Audrey and Dinky so that I could watch all the fun. He played up with the door again. Marcia allowed him to close it a couple of times. But she soon recognized who he was. We had such fun as we carried on our journey to the N.D.A. Percy was a real jovial guy.

When we reached our quarters, he spied a priest's cassock in the dining room. It had just been darned by one of the teachers. Percy picked it up and promptly put it on. It looked as if it was made for him. He made a smashing priest! We called the other teachers to meet 'Father Anthony' from De Nobili College. What a fuss they made over him. He seemed to enjoy it thoroughly. They brought out cake and other goodies, which they had brought from home. Dinky and 'Father Anthony' did full justice to what was offered them.

When the teachers asked him how he managed to be out so late from the Seminary, he replied that he had a late pass. 'Late pass?' I wondered! He was so amusing. I really liked whatever I saw and noticed that night. It did not seem as if we had just met a few hours earlier. In fact, it seemed as if we had known each other for ages. He was such a lovable person and oh! so full of humor. I was attracted towards him... I checked myself. "Thus far and no further, Margaret!"

In the course of that week, Percy went on temporary duty to Barrackpore, near Calcutta. For some reason, he was held up there for a couple of months. Now all I had were a few memories of our first

meeting. I found myself dreaming about him sometimes. I quickly tried to force these dreams out of my
mind. What was I doing dreaming of someone like
this? My dream was to be a nun!

CHAPTER 4

Dreaming by night, thinking by day, all about the same person. But school life continued. I kept myself busy teaching those little children the three 'R's'- Reading! 'Riting! 'Rithmetic! It was cute watching them play and sing. I just loved them. Soon the morning would come to an end. Being the Nursery class teacher, I had only half-day school. As I walked to our quarters, I had time to think and ponder. Percy brought a lot of questions and confusion to my mind. There was an inner struggle. Was I really meant to be a nun? Was that God's plan for me?

I relived the conversation I had with the Lord regarding my love for children. What would I do if I met someone who loved me and vice versa? I loved Percy. There was no doubt about it, but what about my calling? A battle went on within my heart those early days. Was I to become a nun? Or was this dashing young handsome Air Force officer brought into my life for a purpose? The more I came to know him, the more I found he was so loving. He was so full of giving of self. Was **this** the one God had chosen to be the father of my children?

Those days were extremely precious days. I would never exchange those days for anything in the world. Every time I saw Percy, my heart would thud and thump. I could not control it and I wondered if he could hear the loud thumping. He would always cause my heart to beat overtime. I never imagined I could feel like this about anyone. But Percy was not just anyone. He was an extra special one. He was my secret love! He was not aware of my feeling for him. I dared not show him what I felt. I chatted with him when he came over. Laughed at his jokes and pranks. But oh, how I ached inside! I wanted to be absolutely certain, before I revealed my feelings to him.

It was mid-March 1957. Percy came over so excited one evening. "Marge, will you please come for our Air Force Day celebrations on the 31st?" I heard him say to me. "It's our 25th Anniversary on the 1st of April. We are having a special dance this year. Please be my guest Marge."

Should I have been excited with this invitation? Was this going to be an April Fool joke? I had never attended a dance in my life. I felt all the more nervous about going for one now. What would I wear? How would I manage? Would I be able to dance? Countless doubts and questions went through my mind. But with Percy's friendly persuasion and that smile of his, which could melt anyone's heart, I found myself consenting.

There was a lot of discussion with Audrey, regarding what I should wear for this formal occasion. How should I set my hair? Much preparation took place as I waited for this great day.

At last it dawned! My knight in armour came to collect me while Dinky led Audrey to the car. As we came closer to the Mess, I could not believe my eyes. The trees were decked with lights. It was so spectacular. I had never seen anything like this before! Unused to all this pomp and show, I felt like a fish out of water. We walked to our seats as Ken Mac and his band from Bombay played a swing-time favorite. Crowds of people sat on the lawns of No.2 Wing Air Force Officers' Mess.

Percy's family had come from Bombay for this grand ball. I sat and chatted with them. Knowing I had not danced before, I dared not attempt it now. It was good talking to his parents. They were very friendly and charming. I hoped I could pass the night like this. But...there was a far greater hope just around the corner!

Oh! There went the thumping again as I saw Percy approach me. Gallantly he bowed and asked me for the pleasure of the next dance. I felt as if I was walking on a cloud as he led me onto the floor. The band played on. Wait! Was that me? Were those my feet? Gliding from one end of the floor to the other? Wow! We were in step! It was unbelievable! I had never danced before and yet, with music in my veins and with Percy's expert guiding, I found that I enjoyed dancing with him. I never imagined I would dance like this. Like Audrey Hepburn in "My Fair Lady," I could have danced, danced, danced all night. As we danced, we were oblivious to the other couples on the floor. We were the only ones dancing, or so we thought! We were so relaxed. We discussed our families, our work, and our hobbies.

One dance followed another. I wanted it to go on forever. We danced and danced. How often had I met him? How long did I know Percy? Forever! We clicked! The midnight hour was about to strike. Would I have to run away from my Prince Charming? Would I lose my glass slipper? Was this true or was it a dream? No! It was true! Here was Percy by my side, driving us back to the N.D.A. My heart was bursting within. I could hardly speak. Dinky and Audrey were at the back. Percy drove and as he did, he serenaded me. He had such a wonderful voice. "Love me tender, love me true, all my dreams fulfill. For my darling, I love you and I always will...."

Our goodbyes were quick that night. We had to tiptoe into our room. It was late and we could not disturb the other teachers. We grabbed a few hours of sleep and had to face another day of school when we awoke.

Shortly after the Air Force Anniversary, Percy went on a flight to Delhi. Here again, he was delayed. I found myself longing for his return. I wanted to talk to him. I wanted to hear him whisper "Marge" so tenderly. Nobody had ever called me that before. I missed him so much. Those days really dragged.

Till one day I heard the familiar 'Beep Beep' and before I knew it, I looked up and saw his charming smile with those deep dimples. Percy made me feel so great. I enjoyed his visits. I missed him when he did not come. As much as I felt all this, I was still scared to show my feelings for him. I had never, ever had any boyfriends before, whereas Percy had girl-friends. What if...what if...he let me down? I did not want to start a relationship and then be left with a broken heart. How could I be sure? It was so hard. To love and not be able to show it.

Percy had to cover forty miles to see me. It was exactly twenty miles from his Mess at Lohegaon to my quarters at the N.D.A. Even so, he visited me every evening, unless he was on duty. Every time he came, I played it real cool. But how long could this go on? Would he be patient enough to wait? It was evident he had been struck in the same way.

One evening, Audrey and I were invited by Percy and Dinky to their Mess for dinner. They had booked the Ladies' Room. Percy had his choice of records all lined up for the night. The first record he played was: 'We were two innocent hearts.' Yes! I was so very innocent and I had never been in love before. Suddenly, Percy bent down to where I was sitting and gave me a swift kiss on my cheek. I did not think a kiss could be given to any and every one. To me, kissing was very sacred. I dared not return it. He thought I was upset. No, far from it! I just wanted to be certain he was for me and that I was for him.

After dinner we drove to Ramtekdi Hill. This was our 'Blueberry Hill' those days. We drove up to Ramtekdi, where we had a good view of Poona. As I sat with Poona at my feet, he whispered those three magic words. Words, any girl would love to hear, from the person who means the world to her. As elated as I was to hear those words, I was scared to say the same. I knew once I claimed I loved him, it would be sealed. It would be final. I wanted to be absolutely sure and I wanted Percy to be sure as well.

How much he tried. How many times he asked me if I felt anything for him. If only he knew! What was I to say? I told him I could not bear to get hurt. I did not want to love and then lose my love. I knew once I loved, I would love with all I had. My poor Perce. I kept him waiting. But it was worth it! I had to pray much about it. I had to ask God if Percy was the one He had chosen for me. Would he be the father of my children? It did not take much long after that, to find out that I was definitely not going to be a nun; but instead, I would become a NEWNES!

Those days at Khadakwasla were extremely precious. We had many secret haunts in the grounds of the N.D.A. Percy would borrow Dinky's car. As we reached a quiet spot, he would take out a carpet from the dickey and prepare a seat for his 'princess.' Out would come his poetry book. My dear romantic beau would recite poetry to me. I would blush till I could blush no more. "Come Marge, let's go for a picnic tomorrow." He would bring his packed lunch from the Mess and I would get our cook to pack lunch for me.

"What do you want most in the world Marge?" he asked me one day.

"To be happy Perce," I replied.

"Done Marge," said Percy. "I will always make you happy."

And he always did. Percy did not know what it was to be rude or unkind or hurtful. He was the essence of gentleness and kindness. I would be the one to get angry over certain things but Percy was always so cool. He could not even harm a fly.

Soon we had to start planning for our future. With all the serious planning, there would be many light moments as well. I remember vividly Percy taking a large book and sketching out the house of our dreams.

"By the way Marge, how many children should we have?"

"Twelve Perce."

"O.K. I love large families as well. We will have a band of our own, shall we? What say you?"

"Great," I chuckled.

"Now about the rooms," said Percy, deep in thought, as his dimples grew deeper. He sketched them in his plan. "Shall we have six pink rooms and six blue ones?" He was so sure we would play evens! Quite a mansion he had planned ... my dear dear Percy. Each room was sketched with furniture. Dreams, dreams and plans. We enjoyed ourselves playing these make-believe games together.

Percy wanted to save and get me everything before we got married. "We must have a fridge, it is essential. We must get this and we must get that," and I would say, "Oh Percy, if you wait to get all these **things** we will never get married. They are important, no doubt, but we can manage without them."

I made him understand that **things** did not hold an important part in my life. People meant more to me than possessions and he was my 'Percynal

Possession.' I had no idea then just how precious time was.

Thankfully, Percy agreed not to wait too long. When we went home for Christmas, we were engaged. We had our rings blessed in the church and we were committed to God and to each other. We planned to get married the following year.

CHAPTER 5

What a difference it made when I returned to the N.D.A.in January 1958 after a month's vacation in Bombay. I came flashing my engagement ring to all my friends who oohed and aahed. The three diamonds sparkled, but they were put in the shade compared to the sparkle in my eyes! Knowing what the end of the year had in store for me, my joy knew no bounds.

I continued my half-day teaching in the Nursery. Then I would rush back to my room. After lunch, I would start preparing my trousseau. Yvonne, one of the teachers, taught me the basics of dressmaking. Together we prepared my wardrobe. It was so exciting doing this together.

Whenever I went out to town, I would check my list, looking for the essentials to pack away in my bottom drawer. I gathered linen and kitchenware. I had embroidered some tablemats and cushion covers. In the evenings, I kept myself free when my knight in white armour would come from Lohegaon on his 'black steel horse.'

We did a number of trips to Bombay on week-ends. We needed to discuss wedding preparations with our parents. Which church would we marry in? It was decided in the bride's church in Juhu. That was ticked off the list. Who would we invite? The list got longer and longer. Percy's parents, being residents of Bandra for many years, knew countless people. The list was getting so long. If it were left to us, we would have liked to get married in church with an extremely small reception for close relations, but we had to give in.

Next question, "Where would we have the reception?" Everyone thought that Mac Ronnell's Roof Garden was the best place to have it. We contacted the Manager and discussed the menu with him. We decided to have heavy snacks since it was a morning wedding. After the reception, our families would meet at Percy's home for lunch.

I thought that my Perce looked very handsome in his Air Force Blues, so I asked him to get married in his winter uniform. Mum took me to a dressmaker in Bandra. After searching the pattern books, we decided on my dress. It was a full lace dress with tulle frills down the center. As much as Percy wanted to see the pattern we would not allow him to come to the dressmakers. I wanted it to be a complete surprise for him.

The Great Day dawned at last. I could not believe it had arrived. I could not wait to get to the church. Twenty-eighth December nineteen hundred and fifty eight, a day like any other to thousands, but to us, a day we had longed for. At 8.30 a.m. the bells started ringing merrily as my dad walked up the aisle with me to leave me at Percy's side. We glanced at each other coyly and I winked at Percy so lovingly from under the veil, which covered my face.

The service started and soon it was time for us to pronounce our vows together. "For better or worse, for richer or poorer...in sickness and in health, till death do us part." Words mentioned at all wedding ceremonies in church and words that mean so much on that day, but sad to say, people are not always true to these vows. These promises which pledge loyalty to each other, come what may till death, are very often broken.

The church was packed with friends and relations. They were all there to witness our nuptials. I was thrilled to see the wife of General Habibullah (the first Commandant of the N.D.A.) walk in with her daughter Chinky, who was a pupil in my Nursery class. People took trouble to come from far and near to be present on this happy occasion. I cannot recall what the sermon was about that day. Nor can I recall other details. All I know was, that we both looked like a pair of cats who had stolen the cream!

We walked out of the church, wreathed in smiles. Photographs were being taken. Everyone came forward to congratulate us and wish us a long and happy married life. Off we went to the Studio for a group photograph. That completed, we went for a short drive and then wound our way to Mac Ronnells where the guests had assembled and were waiting for us. Johnny Baptista's band was in attendance.

The first song the band played was - 'Two Innocent Hearts.' Was I thrilled! I remembered the first time I heard that song when Percy kissed me in the Air Force Mess. The bridesmaids had two big hearts on which were pinned the favors. "Two innocent hearts" seemed to be the theme of the day.

After a very pleasant morning spent dancing and feasting and meeting all our friends and well-wishers, we went to 'Roseville,' Percy's ancestral home in Bandra. My mother in law and a few relations were on the threshold to welcome us. Percy's mother placed a gold chain round my neck and presented me with two gold bangles. As she did this, rose petals were showered on us. What a great welcome!

There was much music and merriment as the whole clan partook of the sumptuous wedding lunch, which was so lovingly and tastefully prepared by Percy's Mum and sister Lulu. Percy and I did not feel like eating. We were too excited. There was salt tongue and sarpotel. A roasted pigling with its crackling skin lay in the center of the table with an apple in its mouth. There were salads, fried rice and chicken. The table was laden with food. For dessert there was a horn of plenty made of marzipan, nankatais, East Indian thali sweet, coconut sweet, just name it and it was there.

Once lunch was over, there was one thing that I was very keen to do. As tired as we were, Percy consented to drive all the way to Clare Road Convent, the place where I took my Teachers' Training. Off we went in our decorated bridal car to see the nuns. They were so happy to meet us. We were thoroughly surprised when we suddenly heard the strains of the Bridal March being played for us. Percy and I walked up the aisle together.

That chapel held very special memories for me. I had spent many intimate moments with my Creator there. As we reached the front, I placed my bouquet at the foot of the altar. It seemed to have a special significance. I do not really know what, but I felt good doing this.

We came outside and chatted with the nuns. I was glad I could meet them and they could see how happy Percy and I were. We spoke with such openness. They held nothing against me for not becoming a nun. There were fond farewells and then we left for home. We were exhausted. It seemed such a long, long day.

Could we ever forget the 28th December 1958? Never!

The next day we got ready to leave on our honeymoon. What better place to choose than the place filled with memories of our courtship? Father Rehm, my Principal, was only too thrilled to allow us to stay in my room at the N.D.A. Never had this ever happened before and I doubt it ever happened again. We were privileged. 'Black Beauty,' our two-door Morris Minor, brought us just in time to have dinner with Father. After a pleasant chat we bade him goodnight. It was so peaceful there. Time meant nothing to us.

The next morning we heard Father pacing up and down the verandah outside our room. "Oh ho ho ho, oh ho ho ho...Still not up?" An hour later, as we whispered sweet nothings to each other, we could hear the familiar "Oh ho ho" again. Poor Father! He could not imagine why we were not interested in breakfast! We had to inform him later that we would manage breakfast on our own. He should not wait for us. Though we enjoyed his company at the other meals.

After spending a few days there, we proceeded to Mahableshwar, a hill station about a four-hour drive from Poona. 'Black Beauty' proved so faithful to us. We drove wherever we chose during the day. At night, we headed for Kate's Point. 'Black Beauty' was versatile. We turned the seats down and fixed our bedding for the night. It was quite a tight squeeze, half in the dickey and half on the turned down seat. But it was fun! It was a daring adventure and we enjoyed ourselves. Who needed a caravan, when 'Black Beauty' met our every need?

Close to Kate's Point ran a meandering stream. We collected drinking water from there. We jumped into the stream with our swimming costumes and bathed there. Truly, we enjoyed ourselves in this Garden of Eden. Fortunately, it was only on the last day that we noticed buffaloes wallowing in the stream further up. "What the eyes don't see the heart don't feel!" We wondered if they had been there all along!

That morning, a man came selling orchids. He warned us to be careful, as tigers had been spotted roaming in the valley below. It was bad enough seeing buffaloes in our stream, but we did not relish the idea of coming face to face with tigers!

We packed our bags and drove back to Bombay. We decided to spend a few days with each of our families, before it was time for Percy to resume duty in Poona.

It was during our stay in Bombay, that we heard of 'Holiday on Ice.' These ice skaters had come from abroad and were going to perform at the Vallabhai Patel Stadium. We were very keen to see this show. A big gang of us went in four or five cars. Percy had spent the whole day getting the car serviced. After the trip to Khadakwasla, Mahableshwar and then back to Bombay, 'Black Beauty' needed this. Every detail was seen to that day. Percy was so proud of her, as he drove his serviced car to the stadium. We had hardly parked the car, when a young fellow came forward. He assured us he would take care of the car. Out came a yellow duster and he started wiping it. "Good," we said, "the car is in good hands." So we entered the stadium and found our seats. We were all set for an evening of great entertainment.

Amazed and entranced by the skill of these skaters, we were in another world for those few hours. It was an excellent performance. The whole gang left the stadium together. The other cars went ahead. Dad, Sybil and I crossed the road, waiting for Percy to bring our car. What had happened? We wondered! Then suddenly... Percy appeared, with beads of perspiration pouring down his face.

"What's happened Perce? Where is the car?" I asked.

In a choked voice he replied, "The car has gone."

"Oh hon, don't play the fool at this hour. How can it go?"

To that he replied, "It has gone Marge, come and see for yourself."

We crossed the road and found there was no car where it had been parked. We could not believe our eyes. Percy had parked it right in front of a policeman on duty. How could it have happened?

It was nearly 2 a.m. We had to go by taxi to the nearest police station to file a complaint. After leaving Dad and Sybil home at Juhu, we drove to Bandra and shared our news with Percy's family who were extremely shocked. It was difficult to sleep that night, as we were so sad with the loss of our car.

Daily we roamed the highways and byways looking for our car. We were informed that if a car was stolen for spare parts, it could be stripped in a couple of hours. What hope did we have if even a truck could be stripped beyond recognition in a few hours? I told Percy we would buy strong shoes and start walking now that we had no car and no hope of getting it!

I prayed much, begging Jesus for a miracle. Just when we had given up all hope of getting our car, we received a phone call. It was from the police informing us that our car was lying abandoned near Hanging Gardens on Malabar Hill. Our joy knew no bounds. We could not get there fast enough. There was poor 'Black Beauty' robbed of the radio, but there she was, ready to be driven by her owner.

Oh! How we thanked God for answering our prayers. We presumed the boy who volunteered to take care of her, had a skeleton key. He must have opened the car with such confidence that the policeman on duty could not have suspected him at all.

It was a well-known fact, that cars were robbed to carry liquor from place to place. After the job was complete, the stolen car was abandoned by the roadside. Such had been the fate of our 'Black Beauty'. Perhaps someone else had helped himself to our little radio. The main thing was, we had got our car back. If she was special to us before, she was all the more so now.

CHAPTER 6

The days passed and Percy's leave was over. We were due to return to Poona, but there was a snag. We were on the waiting list for family accommodation. This was soon settled when Dinky and Audrey invited us to stay with them. They had an old barrack type of house on T3 Burnett Road, just opposite the big clock tower. We lived out of our trunks. But we did not mind this at all, as long as we were together.

It was fun cooking with Audrey. We would try new recipes to feed our hungry men when they returned home. Not being experts, we always had to have the recipe book open. We did not enjoy cooking on a coal fire. In those days, gas was not heard of in Poona. It was either kerosene or coal.

It did not take long before I could not bear the smoke. I would feel sick with the fumes. Was it only the smoke? I found I was getting sick even when I was not cooking! What could it be? When this carried on for some time, I went with Percy to the doctor. Yes! She confirmed that a miracle was taking place within me. I did not mind what I went through, as long as I knew I had this treasure within.

Our names eventually came on the roster. At long last we were allotted our first home! 95/4 Ghorpuri Married Quarters became our Home Sweet Home. Percy carefully carried me over the threshold. I enjoyed keeping home for Percy. It was exciting to unpack our wedding gifts together and put them to good use.

We made a little garden in the front, and took great delight with our efforts. It was so rewarding to see the plants grow and blossom. It really was like playing 'house house' but now I knew it was not a make-believe game. It was real. It would last forever. There were days when I did not feel inclined to cook. Percy would ask me, "What's for dinner Marge?" I would sit across the table shaking my head and shrugging my shoulders. I would place my fingers at the corners of my eyes. On seeing my slanting eyes, at once my Perce would read my thoughts and knew what I was hinting at.

He would indulge my cravings by taking me to Kamling Restaurant on East Street. That was the only Chinese Restaurant in Poona in those days. It had small private cubicles on one side to sit two to four people in each. We had our favorite room. Invariably, the same steward would attend to us with a big smile on his face. He would watch us study the menu. He knew, however, by this time, that no matter how much we scrutinized the menu, we would always end up with the same order. Sweet corn and chicken soup, mixed fried rice, sweet and sour prawns and

American chop suey. No matter how often we went there, we would always order the same dishes. I would never tire of eating Chinese food. I enjoyed it immensely.

With great excitement I prepared my baby's layette. Everyone asked me whether I was keen to have a girl or a boy. I had no preference. I just wanted a healthy, normal baby. And so I knitted pink and blue sets, embroidered little dresses and blankets. The napkins and sheets were machined. We would make lists of all the necessities required. Together, Percy and I would go out and get all that was needed. Everything was packed and ready. The baby was due on 5th October 1959.

My mother had come down from Bombay prior to my confinement. I felt a strong urgency to pack my suitcase for the hospital on my birthday the 27th September. Percy and Mum raised their eyebrows. What was the hurry? Presumably, it was my sixth sense working overtime. When we got into bed that night, I started to brief Percy about the milkman and the bread man. I went on to explain about the butcher and other details. It was past midnight but I went on with all these details.

YAWN...sigh...yawn! "Marge! What is wrong with you?" asked Percy sleepily. "What is your hurry to tell me all this now? And at this hour? Why can't you tell me this in the morning? The baby is not due for another week . . . Please Marge, please go to sleep darling."... Silence. . .

"Percy?"

"Hmmmmmmm."

SILENCE...toss...turn...

"Percy I think something is happening."

"No no Marge, nothing can happen. It is all your imagination. You are just too tired today. Please Marge, I beg of you, go to sleep and let me sleep."

Silence... I just could not sleep. Something **was** definitely happening. How was I to convince him?

"Percy, Percy come **soon!**" I jumped out of bed and rushed to the toilet as fast as I could. "Percy! Whaaaah...whhaah..." I cried. He found me with tears streaming down my face.

"What has happened Marge? What has happened darling?"

"I think we have lost our baby, Perce." I had started bleeding. I was so upset. Did I go through these nine months just to end it like this? I cried so much. I thought my world would end.

My mother heard the confusion from the next room. Together she and Percy comforted me and prayed for me. Then I dressed and we took my suitcase, which I had packed just hours ago, to the Military Hospital at Wanowrie in our 'Black Beauty'. Fears and doubts kept haunting me. Would everything be all right? Why did this have to happen? How did it happen? What should I do now?

After reaching the Upper Family Ward, I was taken to a side room. Percy and Mum were sent away. I had to spend the night alone. And when I say alone, I mean alone...nobody was there with me. The minutes and hours ticked by as I lay there staring at the walls. It was frightening! How I yearned for my Percy by my side. A nurse would peep in after ages.

She would examine me and say, "Maybe in an hour you will be ready. Try and relax." Another would come later and say, "Don't worry, you have another day to go. Try and sleep." This was getting exasperating. Who was I to believe? An hour? A day? When would it be over?

I could hear the crows cawing in the banyan trees near the parking lot. In the wee hours of the morning, the parish priest came to my bedside and prayed for me. What was that I heard him say? "Come Margaret, make a good confession. Make it like your death bed confession." God forbid! Were they expecting me to die?

As the day staff came on duty, I was taken to a private room with orders to have complete rest. Percy came mid-morning to see how I was progressing. He brought me my favorite book, which I used to refer to during my pregnancy. 'Childbirth without Fear,' by Dr. Grantley Dick Reed. Each time I had a pain, I would study the book to see what was expected of me. Days passed. It did not seem as if there was any progress. What was going to happen? It seemed eternity had passed. At dawn on the 1st October 1959, my membranes ruptured. At last! Something was going to happen that day. Or was it?? I kept on referring to the book. There was nobody else whom I could ask. I kept on breathing, as the book told me I should.

My private maid entered and observed me, so cool and composed. She told me, "You have a long way to go. Nothing is happening yet. You have to scream and pull your hair, then only it will be time."

"Rubbish," I replied. "I am certainly not going to do anything of the sort." I had steeled myself that I would not do anything to hamper the birth of my child. I lay on my bed smiling at each face that literally peeped in and vanished. Seeing me there for the fourth day, they might have wondered how much longer? Percy happened to enter just as I had two very, very sharp pains. "Oh Perce, if these are not the pains, I wonder what they will be like. These are unbearable."

He called a nurse to examine me. She went rushing out and brought a trolley immediately. Evidently, the baby's head could be seen. I was wheeled to the Labour Room. Two nurses were in attendance. They told me to bear down with the next pain. But there were no more pains! I had them alone in the room. Nothing seemed to happen. As I tried, I could hear these two nurses discussing me. They were making up their minds to send me to the Operation Theatre. I was doing my best, but there were no more pains!

"Tell me what I am to do. Help me please," I pleaded with them. I prayed and bore down with all the strength left in me. "Carry on carry on," the nurses encouraged me. : "Oh Lord, help me," I prayed. It seemed impossible. Again I tried and tried. How very much I tried. I was rewarded when at long last; my ears heard the most beautiful sound; the sound of my newborn baby's cry. "Congratulations! You have a girl," said the nurses in unison. "Give her to me please. I want to hold her," I said. At once, the maternal instinct was at work within me.

"Hello Cheryl Ann," I cooed as I cradled her in my arms. Forgotten was the pain and anxiety I had been through. I was amazed to see that she looked the image of her Dad. Wouldn't he be proud! Even the way she winked at me and turned her mouth sideways, as her Dad would do in fun. I was overjoyed.

You should have seen the proud father when he arrived minutes later with my mother, after being informed of the birth of our daughter. Our joy was complete.

Our whole schedule changed once we took Cheryl home. If anyone visited us during the day, they would have been unaware that there was a baby in our home. She slept so soundly most of the day. Let night come! I could count the hours I paced the floor with Cheryl. She was a regular night bird from birth and she has not changed much even now!

Between cooking and other household chores, I would try and snatch some sleep. Our whole world revolved around our baby. It was with such joy we watched Cheryl grow. Her first smile . . . the way she discovered her fingers and toes... crawling, turning, trying to sit, then stand. Her first tooth, her first steps. Each new phase brought excitement to us.

Now we had a new book to refer to... Dr. Spock's book was said to be the last word in childcare. A little rash, extra stools, hiccoughs, and straightaway we would look up the index and see what Dr. Spock had to say. It was the last word for us. Relations and friends would come and say, "Well, I think you should do this." And quick would come the reply, "No! But Dr. Spock says this." And that was final. He had the last word in our home as far as the bringing up of our baby was concerned.

Cheryl was hardly seven or eight months when Percy had to go on a trip to the Nicobar Islands. I had started expecting our second child. Being alone at home, I took it easy and hardly cooked. I kept myself busy looking after Cheryl, stitching and gardening. I used to carry buckets of water to tend to the garden. All this had a bad effect on me. Something went wrong somewhere. I started bleeding and had severe pain. I had to put the brakes on. There was Cheryl, myself and only a part-time servant at home. It was not really possible to have complete rest.

"Percy," my heart cried out, " if only you were here, I would feel better." But there was no way of getting through to him, while he was on duty at the Andaman and Nicobar Islands. I soon realized it was more dangerous than I had imagined. I just lay at home by myself till Providence brought a friend to visit me. She was so shocked to see me suffering. Immediately, she brought a rickshaw and took me to the Medical Mission Sisters' Dispensary, which was on Center Street. The doctor examined me and confirmed that I had to have complete rest.

Percy returned from his trip and was aghast when I told him what I had been through in his absence. The next morning, he took me to the Military Hospital for a check up. We were informed that I had already had a miscarriage. Perce was so loving and caring. He felt so bad that he was not with me when I went through this traumatic experience.

Life went on as usual for some time. Having had a miscarriage at such an early stage of pregnancy, I did not feel I had lost a baby. I had Cheryl to fill my hours. But after a few months, I was longing to have another baby. With each month that passed, I found I was not pregnant. I started worrying. Would I ever be able to have a baby after the miscarriage? I felt so wretched. After waiting for a year, I told Percy if I did not get pregnant the following month, I was going to adopt a baby. God knew how much I longed for another baby. By the following month, another miracle took place in my womb. I was overjoyed.

I was about four months pregnant, when Percy received his posting orders from Poona. Fortunately, it was not too far away. We were posted to the N.D.A. How excited we were. Back were we going to the place, which held so many memories for us.

We had to close our house at Poona. Everything was packed and loaded in a truck. We were extremely happy about this posting. We were allotted a beautiful house overlooking the lake. To the back of the house, was a high hill.

It was not long before Father Rehm, principal of the school, came over on a business visit. He asked me if I would teach again. This time, I taught Std.III. I continued to teach there till a fortnight before the baby's date of arrival.

I used to go for periodic check-ups at the N.D.A. hospital and all seemed fine. Somehow at the end, the doctor panicked and insisted that I be admitted to the Command Hospital in Poona in case of an emergency. There was no need for alarm. I had a normal delivery. My mother was with me. She was a real source of help. They even allowed her in the Labour Room and this made all the difference. With her guidance and help, Robin William announced his arrival on the 30th November 1961.

Percy was ecstatic to know he now had a son. That grin of his was enough to tell me what was on his mind. He was thinking of a partner to share in his weight-lifting sessions. To say nothing of teaching him the trumpet! While we were rejoicing at the birth of our son, Percy's father was admitted to hospital in Bombay. He had undergone an operation and was rather serious. Poor Perce, did not know which side to turn. Since Mum was with me, I asked to be discharged from hospital on the third day after Robin was born.

On returning home to be with Cheryl, I encouraged Percy to go to Bombay to be with his father for some time. Percy's Dad recovered and went home after a short stay in hospital. Percy came back home to us at Khadakwasla.

I was delighted with our two children. Each day brought added pleasure as I noticed new developments in them.

But suddenly, I was getting 'sick' again! Robin was hardly three months old and another baby was on the way! Real quick work! On top of it, we received news of Percy's posting to Barrackpore, near Calcutta. It was quite a feat packing home this time. In between I had to see to Cheryl's and Robin's needs. At last, all the packages were stitched and labeled. We just had to wait for the day of departure.

Then one fine day Percy came home with news that he had been selected to go to Russia to be trained on AN 12 Russian transport aircraft. I had mixed feelings. There was I with two infants and expecting the third and Percy brings this news of his going so far away. On the other hand, I was happy because Percy was so excited at this wonderful opportunity. It just shows we can plan and yet, can we be sure these plans will materialize? Here was our entire luggage labeled 'From Poona to Barrackpore' and now it was goodbye to Barrackpore and goodbye to Khadakwasla also.

Instead of Barrackpore, Percy had to report to Poona and be on standby till the Russian trip materialized. Once again, we had no quarters, but were fortunate to shift into a friend's house at Lohegaon as they had proceeded on leave. We lived like nomads. It was pointless unpacking.

Cheryl had helped me in caring for Robin, who was ten months old now. I needed all the help I could get. I grew tired as my pregnancy progressed. We hardly saw Percy at this time. The pilots used to come and go at odd times. Aircraft thundered across the sky both by day and night. War was declared with China. What happened to 'Hindi-Chini bhai bhai '?

I used to wait anxiously for Percy's return each time he went on a sortie. He, on the other hand, was worried about me. He told me that each time he went on a sortie, he worried in case I would need medical assistance and he couldn't get to me when I needed him. What would happen to Cheryl and Robin? All these thoughts kept flashing in his mind. So he requested me to please go to Bombay and stay with my parents. As hard as it would be for us to be separated he said he would be at peace. It was difficult saying goodbye. We wanted to cherish every possible moment with each other, especially since he had to leave for Russia in a short time.

Daily, we read in the newspapers of the many people who had come to a bitter end due to this nasty war. One day, Percy asked me what would I do if he met his end like them. I just would not hear of it. I refused to believe or accept this could happen to my Percy. After all, had we not planned to live till a ripe old age together with our dozen children? All the same, he asked me to be very brave in case anything happened to him. He asked me to take care of our three children for his sake. Even though I did not want to think of something happening to Percy, I promised him if the need arose I would work and take care of our children. I promised...yet I hoped and prayed I would always have Percy by my side.

I had to eventually leave for Bombay with the children. We could not stay together in Poona any longer. Whenever it was possible, Percy would drop in for a few hours to see us. Then it was back to Poona for him. The pilots were worked off their feet and had to be alert and ready to fly at short notice.

It was a strange feeling not having Percy with me as the date of our baby's arrival drew nigh. On the other hand I counted it a blessing to be home for this delivery. Dr. Leggett and his wife Marjorie were going to deliver their grandchild. How different it was being at home rather than in a hospital.

With each pain I had, Mum made me walk the floor. She kept on encouraging me. Eventually you could hear me saying, "It's coming! It's coming." We had to literally run to my bedroom. Dad was woken from his sleep. With no trouble whatsoever, our baby Patricia Angela was born on the 22nd December 1962 just after one o'clock in the morning!

How my heart cried out for Percy. He missed a wonderful opportunity of actually being present at the birth of our child. They phoned him as soon as they could and Percy flew to Bombay to see us. He could not even spend a night with us. He came, he saw, and he had to return to Poona.

Duty called him back!

CHAPTER 7

It was sad having Percy's baby and not having him with me to enjoy her. He was not able to stay a day longer after seeing little Patricia. After receiving instructions and a briefing in Poona, Percy had to proceed to Delhi. He spent a short time there and then left for Russia with his course mates in January 1963. How we missed each other. We longed for the day when we would be together again. I did not know what God was trying to teach me through this long separation. It was only our daily letters to each other that kept us in touch.

He was keen to know about his babes. I used to fill my letters with details: Patricia's first tooth, Robin's first steps, Cheryl's first day at Nursery School. He missed out on all these things. We just kept counting the days for his return, so that we could be together as a family again.

At last six months passed and Percy returned to Delhi. From there, he got his posting orders to Chandigarh in the Punjab. He could not wait to see us and we to be with him. He wrote and asked me to come immediately to join him, as his leave could not be sanctioned straightaway. As much as I wanted to be with my Perce, I knew I would never manage traveling with our three babies alone. I would have to look after them plus the luggage, and then change trains at Delhi. I could not possibly do it alone, so I had to wait for Percy to come for us.

Before coming to Bombay, Percy had to arrange for a house. Since the Air Force Station at Chandigarh was fairly new, there were no Air Force Quarters. Civilian houses in town were rented to the service officers. Percy managed to get a really good one. It was most spacious and well located, just behind the famous Tagore Theatre in Sector18. He drew out the plan and sent it to me. It was a three-bedroom house with a very large sitting-cum-dining room. There was a large compound and the exciting addition was the terrace. This was a boon as most families slept on their terraces in the Punjab, because of the intense heat.

Leave was sanctioned and Percy came to Bombay to take us to our 'Home Sweet Home'. We had fare-well meals with all our relations. At last the day came for us to be together again. It was on July 2nd 1963. On our way to the station, Percy held my hand and asked me if I was happy. Our eyes met and locked in a loving embrace. I replied, "I couldn't be happier, my Perce. It is so good to be with you again. Please darling, please promise me that you will never leave me again...never."

Percy, continuing to look me in the eye said, "I will never leave you again Marge darling, never- as I too cannot live without you." I believed my Perce as always. I can remember the place so vividly where this conversation took place. It was just as the taxi was approaching the Mosque at Bandra.

We soon reached Victoria Terminus. Babes and luggage were all under control as we mingled with the crowd. We headed for the Frontier Mail and looked up the passenger list. We were allotted a coupe. We settled our luggage and ourselves as best as we could. As the train shunted out of Bombay, I gave Cheryl and Robin their dinner and soon they were in the Land of Nod. Little Patricia had to be fed and slept in my arms.

The next morning, the children awoke full of excitement. This was their first long journey and they thoroughly enjoyed every moment of it. I cannot say the same about me. I suppose it was the anxiety of seeing to the major part of the packing on my own, besides taking care of the children, the excitement of being reunited with Percy, plus the intense heat. It all added up to my feeling sick. Every now and then, I would dash to the toilet to throw up. I would hardly settle down, when off I would charge again.

I can still picture Percy standing at the door of our coupe, biting his lower lip. This was so characteristic of him. He shook his head vigorously saying, "Poor, poor Marge. You are more fertile than a rabbit!"

Oh no! I know we wanted our twelve children. But right now I felt I needed a respite. Having had three children and one miscarriage in quick succession, I felt I needed to have a break. It did not take me long to realize that it was only the heat and tiredness that had caused me to feel so sick.

Dawn broke over Chandigarh as we arrived on the small platform. It was quite a difference to Bombay and Delhi. Dinky came to the station in his black Ambassador. (The same one in which I first met Percy.) He drove us to our new home. I was taken aback by the cleanliness of Chandigarh and the expert way in which this town had been planned. We drove past the Tagore Theatre, down a narrow lane and right again. Then straight-- till we arrived at 39 C Sector 18 B our 'home sweet home.'

In our modern spacious house I took great delight in unpacking and making our home liveable and welcome. It was so rewarding because Percy was appreciative of everything I did. Daily he would come home and appreciate my feeble efforts with such encouragement. Our home was really taking shape. At night, we would carry our bedding up to the terrace and sleep there. As refreshing as it was, we could not continue in this way for very long, as we used to be plagued by flies. They were worse than an alarm clock. Swarms of flies would hover around us and rudely awaken us much too early from our slumber.

Percy needed to have a good sleep at night, as he was kept very busy at work. His squadron used to carry supplies in their large transport planes daily. They had to fly over Leh and Ladakh and drop supplies in the valleys below. They needed to be precise and careful as they flew between the hazardous mountain ranges. There was so much more to study about these aircraft. Not only did his squadron fly by day, they also had night flying. It was imperative they kept alert and well.

'Black Beauty' arrived a week after we did. We were informed of her arrival by the Railway authorities. There was great excitement as Percy brought her home from the station. As a treat, Percy used to drive us round the town in the evenings. Chandigarh was a well-planned city with colossal buildings. Each house was better than the other. I would point to a real beauty and say "Perce, let us build our house in Poona like this one."

And he would say, "No Marge no."

"Why Perce? Why can't we have a house like that? Don't you like it?"

"Of course it is nice Marge, but the house I plan for you, will be much better than all these houses put together."

And that was final. I knew I did not have to pursue the matter. I knew if my Perce planned it, it would be good. Plans . . .plans… again and again. How much we planned. Can you be sure of the plans you make? Will they materialize? There is only One who can plan and be certain those plans will come to pass.

On the 13th July 1963, as we were having lunch together, Percy and I discussed the day's happenings. The children were asleep. As I watched him I could sense how tired he was. He mentioned it was very tense work. They had to be extremely careful whilst flying, but he enjoyed it all the same. He just loved flying.

My next question must have taken him by surprise. "Do you pray before you take off Percy? I mean, do you make the sign of the cross in front of the others? Do you proclaim you are a Christian?" Before I could go further, his reply astounded me.

"I talk quietly to Jesus," he said.

"Talk?" I reiterated. "How do you talk? Don't you say three Hail Mary's and the Act of Contrition?"

"No Marge, I just talk to Jesus and ask Him to take care of me and keep me safe and I ask Him to take care of you and the babies." His reply alarmed me. In fact, it had me floored. I was the religious one but I did not know how to **talk** to Jesus!

The way Percy told me this, it was so child-like. Here was I expecting him to perform outward mechanical demonstrations, but what Percy said, made me think. There was such a depth of meaning in what he got across to me. God wants us to be simple and childlike when we come to Him. Even as a pilot and the father of three children he would say this prayer with childlike faith and trust and simplicity.

"Jesus tender Shepherd hear me
Bless Thy little lamb tonight.
Through the darkness be Thou near me
Keep me safe till morning light.
Let my sins be all forgiven
Bless the friends I love so well
Take me when I die to Heaven
Happy there with Thee to dwell."

Surprising! It was the first time I heard this prayer when Percy had recited it.

July 16th 1963 dawned like any other day. Percy rose bright and early. He had his regular flying sortie over Ladakh and Leh. He dropped his supplies to the waiting troops and returned home earlier than usual. Surprised, I asked how he had managed to come home so soon. He said that they allowed him home early, as he was scheduled to return for night flying.

After our lunch and a short nap, Percy got down to fix the radio for me. "What is your hurry Perce? Leave the radio alone. You can always do it some other time." But he seemed determined to complete it that particular day.

"I must do it Marge. I want you to have music especially when I am out." In the bargain, he cut his finger and it started bleeding. I rushed to get a band-aid to seal the cut. He looked at me lovingly and said, "First class Marge," and I said, "Hope I will always be first class for you my darling."

He was thrilled when the radio was fixed and in working order. I looked at the clock. It was time to serve his dinner. As I was walking out of the kitchen with the dinner, I nearly dropped it. Together we heard the strains of 'Night and Day' come over the air. This was a song held in superstition by the Air Force. It was a bad omen. We looked across that large room. Percy, still near the radio and I, in the kitchen doorway. Our eyes locked. How much I wanted to cry out in anguish and plead with him not to fly that night. I wanted to say, "Can't you hear that song Perce? You know what it means?" I wonder if Percy had the same thoughts. Who knows?

On second thoughts, I knew it would be pointless being superstitious and warning him. It would only have a bad effect on him. So I kept quiet. I tried to act normal and make small talk but that song went on and on in my mind. Why did *that* song have to come over the air? Why did he have to repair the radio just today? Why? Why?

"Get a hold of yourself Margaret Newnes," I said to myself and cleared the table. Percy got ready to leave. We went to see him off at the gate. Our good-byes lingered. The children took turns to kiss him. Each time they kissed him, I would say, "Last kiss for Mummy." This went on and on. But with the last and final kiss, I had to eventually let him go.

CHAPTER 8

After Percy left, we came inside. I undressed the children and we got together to say our prayers.

"Gentle Jesus meek and mild
Look upon this little child.
Pity me and pity my simplicity;
Suffer me to come to Thee.
Heart of Jesus I adore Thee,
Heart of Mary I implore thee
Heart of St. Joseph pure and just,
In these three hearts I place my trust."

Then would come a whole list of people we would ask God to bless and end the prayer asking God to bless each one of us and make us good, loving and obedient.

My Mum taught these prayers and others to me and I, in turn, taught them to my children. We said three Hail Mary's, which we had to say morning and night. Then we asked Jesus to keep Daddy safe and bring him back soon.

I tucked them in bed and tried to creep away. "Mama," they called out, "please tell us a story." I obliged by telling them 'The Three Bears.' Even as I was narrating it, they dropped off to sleep. At about 9.43 p.m. I heard the drone of the AN12. Knowing that Percy's flight was till 9.45 p.m. I rejoiced, excited to know he would be home in about half an hour.

I waited and waited, but there was no sign of Percy. I paced up and down, waiting and watching, watching and praying. But all I could hear in the stillness of the night was the awful howling of dogs. Was this a superstitious sign? When I was in boarding school in Yercaud, and we heard a dog or hyena howl at night, it was always associated with the herald of bad news. Would I receive bad news of someone in the family?

Strange, on this particular night, even though Percy was so late in coming home, I had no fear at all about him. I knew my Perce would return. I continued to wait, pacing up and down. It was soon midnight. I could hear the distant chimes strike the midnight hour. And still, there was no sign of Percy. By this time, I presumed something had happened to his scooter. I sent my servant to Dinky's house to enquire if he knew the cause of the delay.

Audrey and Dinky stayed not far from us. Percy's and Dinky's Commanding officer and his wife were staying with Dinky. I had informed Dinky that Percy's sortie was till 9.45 p.m. and it was now past midnight and he had not yet come home. I mentioned that his scooter might have been giving him trouble. He sent word that there had been an accident, but he assured me that it was not Percy's aircraft. Knowing that Dinky must have received this information from the C.O. I tried to relax and wait patiently.

I could picture Percy lending a helping hand to those who were hurt. Poor Perce. He was so tired himself. What a long day he had. When would my Perce return? I tried to settle myself but could not really rest till I saw him. There was no fear, none at all. But I just could not dream of sleeping till my Percy came home. This was my habit. I would always wait for my beloved whether he flew by day or by night.

I heard the clock strike one o'clock. I heard it strike two. There was still no sign of Percy. All I could hear was the continuous howling of dogs in the stillness of the night. I paced up and down between the toilet and the verandah. I looked at our children. They were fast asleep. Cheryl and Robin in their room. Little Patricia lay in her bed next to mine. Back again I went outside and paced. Praying...wondering...when oh when would my Percy come home?

It was about 2.30 a.m. I saw two bright lights heading down the road towards our home. It was not our scooter. Perhaps...it was Percy who was wounded? Perhaps not! As the car stopped, I saw Audrey alight first.

What was **she** doing in the car? I expected Percy. Was everything O.K.? Where was Percy? Four others alighted from the car. But there was still no Percy. What could have happened? I ran out of the gate towards the car, looking for my Perce. "Where is he? Where is my Percy?" All they said was, "We are sorry. We are so sorry." Sorry for what? Sorry for whom? Was Percy dead? It couldn't be! I had been told very clearly that it was not Percy's aircraft. Then what were they sorry about? It just would not dawn on me.

When it eventually hit me, I pleaded with them to take me to his side. I wanted to kiss him once more. I wanted to whisper a prayer in his ear. Even at that moment, my mind traveled back to my Catechism class in school. Even if someone died, we could whisper the 'Act of Contrition' in that person's ear two to three hours later. I sincerely believed what I had been taught. So I wanted to whisper this prayer in Percy's ear asking God to forgive him his sins.

As much as I pleaded to be taken to Percy, they kindly yet firmly refused. They told me to try and visualize him as I last saw him. They told me to remember his smiling face. They wanted me to have happy memories of him. I learned later that all six of them in the aircraft were burned beyond recognition.

It was all a nightmare.

I could not believe it was true.

How could it happen to me?

Why did it have to happen?

'Night and Day'? -------- Howling dogs?

A few more Air Force Officers and their wives came trickling into my house in the early hours of the morning. I was completely stunned. I was shocked. I was in a daze. It could not be true. No it was! I felt I was taking part in a big drama.

I offered these good people tea, at that unearthly hour. Of course they did not accept the tea but stayed for some time to offer me some comfort. I did not know half the people, as we were new to the Station. We had just been there for twelve days. By coming at that time, they showed they cared. They felt one with me in my time of sorrow.

After some time they left. Audrey stayed on. I went inside to have a peep at my children. Little Patricia, just six and a half months was fast asleep in her bed. She was unaware of what had happened. She had known her Dad for exactly a fortnight and now he was no more. There lay Robin, my one and a half year old son, sucking his pacifier, the only man in our family.

Cheryl, my eldest happened to get up just then. She entered the room twirling her favorite 'blank-a-let.' "Mama, where's Daddy?" she asked. I, still in shock replied, "Darling, Daddy has gone to Heaven to be with Jesus. He will never come back again." What that little three-and-a-half year old understood, I would not know. But she turned right around, walked back to her bed and fell into a deep sleep. I was too shocked.

I could not even shed a tear.

CHAPTER 9

Sleep would not come at all. I realized I had not shut my eyes at all that dreadful night. The night of 16th July that continued to the early morning of July 17th. Telegrams were sent to Bombay to Percy's parents in Bandra and my parents in Juhu. It would be a great shock to them. Exactly a fortnight ago we had wished them goodbye. Had they any premonition it would be the final goodbye? I doubt it!

Percy's sister Freda and her husband Tony were posted at the Air Force Station Delhi. They were contacted by phone. They said they would come as soon as possible.

The darkness of the 16th night ebbed away as the sun rose heralding a new day. What did that day bring for me? There was a huge vacuum and emptiness in my heart. Mechanically, I helped the children to dress. My heart was so heavy. As I passed through Percy's dressing room, my eyes fell on his uniform, which I had so lovingly laid out for him the previous night.

I touched those empty clothes, but that is just what they were. Empty clothes with no Perce to get into them. I traced my footsteps through every room trying to capture memories. I hoped I could get my Percy back. If only they had come and said he was "Missing"------ But ------- DEAD! DEAD!

There was no hope at all. To the dining room, I retraced my footsteps. The breakfast table was laid for two. We used to have our breakfast very early before Percy left for duty. The tablemats, which I had embroidered with such joy for my bottom drawer, lay there. I shook myself back to reality. My children needed to be fed. "Come darlings, come and eat," I called to them. What did they understand about what had happened? Cheryl might have felt it. Robin and Patty were too small to realize anything. Besides Daddy had been away in Russia for so long and then he had come back. They might have thought he would come back to us again.

I kept my babes with the servant as Audrey and I had to go and meet the parish priest. We informed him of Percy's death. I arranged with him to offer a Mass for Percy's soul. The funeral arrangements had to be discussed with him as well. Father was very kind and sympathetic. Audrey and I returned home with heavy steps and heavier hearts. Even though plans were made, I still could not believe it was true. All other details were attended to by the Air Force. They were seeing to the coffin and all the other Service funeral arrangements.

It suddenly dawned on me to search through my cupboard for something to wear for Percy's funeral.

There was a snazzy black dress with a heavy lace collar. Percy had brought this especially for me to wear at a Mess function. I could not possibly wear this today. Oh! There was the white sharkskin suit I had - another party outfit, which my Perce had not even seen me in. That too was kept aside. At last I found a dress befitting for my beloved's funeral.

As I was ironing my dress, my thoughts were wandering. To think I had just completed unpacking everything only the day before. I did not relish the idea of packing all this again. What a contrast it would be compared to the excitement I went through packing to come to Chandigarh just to be with my Perce.

Audrey and Dinky brought lunch over. The Commanding Officer and his wife together with the Parish priest came as well. I just could not eat at all. I kept drinking tea throughout the day. My thoughts went to Percy all the time. I wondered where my Percy was. If only I could see him.

The Air Force had made six coffins out of packing cases and painted them black. The coffins were laid out in the morgue in the civil hospital at Sector 23.

After lunch and a rest, Cheryl, Robin and Patty were taken to Audrey's house, to be with her children, while we got ready for the funeral.

The Air Force personnel were lined up outside the hospital as the staff car drove in with Audrey, Dinky and me. I saw the pallbearers coming up the slope from the morgue carrying Percy's coffin on their shoulders. It was a hot and sultry afternoon. Not a leaf stirred. I felt hotter as I stood there. I heard the chimes of a distant clock strike four.

Soon we would be on our way to the Christian cemetery far out in Sector 32. It was a fairly new cemetery with very few graves. I heard when Chandigarh was planned they had not even thought of one. Then one of the architects died suddenly and so this one was quickly developed.

Percy was the only Christian who had died in the accident. The others were Hindus and Muslims. They had been buried according to their religious rites. Now, this was really going to be the end for Percy, my beloved.

CHAPTER 10

As I entered the cemetery, I was thankful that the children had not come with me. I was grateful that they were so young and did not understand what had really happened. Yet, on second thoughts, would I have been happier if they were older? They would be able to stand with me and by me in this time of deep sorrow. True, friends and well-wishers were there. But it would surely have been better to have my three loved ones. Honestly, I felt I was taking part in a play. It was totally unreal.

I stood up near the freshly dug grave with Audrey by my side. All the Air Force and Army officers had come dressed in their uniforms with ribbons and medals. The parish priest read the funeral prayers. I cannot recall a single word he said. My thoughts were only with my Perce who lay in that box at my feet. That black box was draped with the National flag. Above that lay Percy's peak cap.

As the sun was slowly setting in the western sky, the officers walked up in single file. Each one smartly saluted the coffin. It seemed never-ending.

When would this end? It made me feel elated to see Percy having all this respect. It did not seem like a mere facade. It seemed to come straight from their hearts. Right from the Generals down to other ranks, all came and paid their respects to my Percy, as I stood aside and watched.

Just before they lowered the coffin, I bent down and Audrey grabbed me and tried to pull me back. I had only bent to take Percy's cap, the only visible remains of my Percy. She might have thought I wanted to jump in the grave as well. I told her not to worry. I would never do such a thing. Where would it get me? I had my three little ones to care for. What good would it do even if that thought had entered my mind? After all, those were only the charred remains of my loved one. I had to live for my Cheryl, Robin and Patty. Like a flash, I remembered Percy asking me to take care of them if anything would happen to him. Did I dream it would happen so soon? NEVER!

The loud, heart-rending boom of the guns then broke the silence. This is typical of any Service funeral when the 21-gun salute is given. The bugler played the Last Post. Even that, touching as it sounded, could not bring tears to my eyes. I was in a daze. I stood there, but how dead I felt within.

Before the earth was fully turned, Audrey gently drew me away. How swiftly that Great Romance had come to an end. I recalled we were only married for four and a half years. Out of that time, Percy had been in Russia for six months. He went there with much excitement to train on AN 12 s, and it was in one of those aircraft that he met his end.

The Air Force car took me to Audrey and Dinky's house. My children were unaware of what had happened and where I had gone. After caressing them, I was taken to a room to rest after the nightmarish 'Night and Day.' I could not sleep. I could not even close my eyes. I just lay there, staring into space. I could hear everyone talking in the next room.

They were concerned that I had not cried at all. I asked for a cup of tea and for my children. I hugged them to me. They were all I had now. If only I could tell them what had happened. But I could not...I would not. Dinner was served. I refused that also.

As dinner was served, Freda, Percy's eldest sister and her husband Tony, arrived from Delhi. They were delayed on the way, so could not make it in time for the funeral. Even though they were late, it was great seeing them. They had a special place in our hearts as we spent much of our courting days in their home at Poona, while they were posted there.

Audrey asked me to sleep in her house that night. I politely declined the offer. I wanted to go to our home, even with those memories. I entered 39 C. I walked again through all the rooms as if in a dream. I stroked Percy's clothes still lying there. No more would I set out his clothes for him. There was no Percy. My life seemed to have ended.

A spark had burned out.

CHAPTER 11

Our life in Chandigarh had come to an abrupt end within twelve days of us having arrived. The children and I had to move. But move where? My parents had invited me to make our home with them in Juhu. So did my in laws in Bandra. I thought it would be wiser to face life on my own with my children.

Vera and Tony Mousinho, good friends of ours and godparents of Patty, drove down from Halwara, an Air Force base north of Chandigarh. They had just written to us on the 16th July, asking if they could spend a weekend with us. What a different trip this turned out to be for them!

All the same, they came to be with me in my time of grief. They invited us to their home for a few weeks. Those few weeks turned into a few months. Tony and Vera were very kind to us. They let us do whatever we wished. We went out for long walks together. They understood if I wanted to speak or if I wished to be silent. They were so accommodating.

Both Vera and Tony left each day for work. He was a pilot and she, a teacher. Their children would also leave for school. That left my children and me alone. Before leaving for work, they would instruct the servant to see to our every need. In the afternoon, when they returned, they would take us out for drives.

Often we would go to the canal close by to fish. Another great pastime was to play 'Scrabble.' This was a reminder of our foursome at Khadakwasla. Now there were just three of us.

It was a fortnight since we had arrived in Halwara. To respect my feelings, Tony and Vera had refrained from playing any music. An Air Force friend came over that day and wanted to hear one of their records. Many signs and glances went on between them. I could hear muffled whispers. It was only then did I realize there was no music for the past fortnight, because of me. I told them to go ahead and play the record.

I did not know which record their friend wanted to hear. But as Benny Goodman came over the air and the strains of 'Memories of You' hit me, I felt so ashamed of myself. I found I could not sit there another second. I rushed out of the room and into the bedroom. I dived headlong onto the bed.

For the first time since Percy's death I cried and cried. All the pent-up feelings came out. The flood-gates were opened. This was a tune, which Percy had mastered so well on his trumpet after hours and days of practice. All those memories of him practicing the trumpet behind closed doors came to my mind. I remembered both of us playing together as in a flash-back. He on the trumpet and me on the piano. The shock had now turned to tears. I felt much better for it, but Tony and Vera felt bad. They could not stop apologizing to me. But it was a good release that I had been building up within.

As good as my friends were, we certainly could not stay with them indefinitely. So at the end of three months, we returned to Chandigarh by bus. It was a long, hot, tiring journey. In Chandigarh, I had to collect what was left of my earthly belongings. Before leaving for Halwara, I had asked Dinky and Audrey to keep me the bare essentials to run my home and to sell the rest of my possessions. Extra plates, dishes, vases, curios and things I did not think I would need, were to be disposed of. I had no intention of ever entertaining again, so I asked them to have a sale.

I was glad to be saved the agony of breaking up my home. Dinky and Audrey took good care of this for me. I decided to spend a few days in Chandigarh before going to Delhi to be with Freda and Tony. While in Delhi, I had to settle about my pension at Air Headquarters. It was not clear what I should do or where I should go. Should I teach in Delhi? In Bombay? Where should I apply for a job? I still was not aware of the One who plans for us and holds our past, present and future in His hands.

I applied to the Frank Anthony School in Delhi. Being an Anglo Indian, I was certain I would have a chance there. However, I drew a blank. I applied to Bishop's School in Poona and received a nega-tive reply, even though I knew the Principal. After all, nobody wanted the risk of taking a twenty five year old widow with three tiny children to work for them.

The next place I applied to was the Convent of Jesus and Mary in Poona. I was offered a job for Rs.130/-per month. How would I ever bring up my children on this meagre amount? The nuns were very kind. They said they would give me tuitions to help out. Nothing seemed clear. If I agreed to teach at the Convent and supplement the income with tuitions, how much time would I have with my children who needed me? I did want to be a good mother to them. So I refused that job. I had to sacrifice one important value-the children's education in a Catholic school to a greater value to me at that time, spending time with my children.

I then heard of a vacancy in St. Mary's Poona and so I applied there. This was an Anglican School. Sr. Susan Dominica the Principal replied to me. She added a P.S. "Are you a Roman?" On receiving an affirmative reply from me, she promptly wrote and told me that the vacancy had been filled. Que sera! What was I to do? Where should I go? I had to work... but where?

Despondent and depressed, worrying about my future, I recall lying down one afternoon. We were alone in our bedroom in Dinky and Audrey's house. There I lay thinking...worrying...reflecting. How would I manage to bring up my wee ones? They had their whole lives ahead of them. How would I manage? Surely there was some way.

And then came a Voice. "Build a house and have a Nursery." Huh? Who was speaking? There was nobody else in the room except my children. Again a second time, the Voice came loud and clear. "Build a house and have a Nursery." I knew this was God speaking to me. I then remembered the plot we had registered in our names in St. Patrick's Town Poona. Percy had given a small down payment for it. I did not think I would be able to pay the remaining amount. Nor did I dream I would be able to build a house. And here, was this Voice so clearly telling me I should build a house **and** have a Nursery.

"Knock knock, postman," said Dinky as he entered my room and handed me a letter. It was from the parish priest who had sold us the plot of land. He happened to be the Chairman of St. Patrick's Town Committee. I tore open the letter. "Why don't you build a house and have a Nursery?" he wrote. You could have knocked me down with a feather when I read that. If I had received the letter and then heard the Voice, I would have thought it was my imagination working overtime. Or it might have been a coincidence. But this…this was too much to digest. I knew this was what God wanted. How and when I did not know. But if it were God's plan for me, He would surely make it possible.

The priest went on to say in his letter that he would get me a loan from Germany to build my house. He had also contacted Ronnie, a Christian contractor to build my house at a concession. Now there was something to look forward to. When God closes a door, He opens a window.

The time had come for us to say goodbye to Chandigarh. As we were getting ready to leave, the morning post arrived. I was surprised to receive a letter from Sr. Susan Dominica of St. Mary's School, Poona. She commenced the letter by saying that she was writing to Chandigarh, Delhi and Bombay; to make sure I would receive the letter in time. She knew I would be on the move, as I had given her these forwarding addresses.

Sr. Susan mentioned that the teacher, who had previously filled the vacancy, was unable to join St. Mary's. She asked if I was still available and would I consider teaching in her school from January 1964. Would I consider? What a question! Now things seemed brighter. It was good receiving this news. The salary offered was Rs. 236/- per month, but in 1964, it seemed good enough. God was definitely guiding me to Poona.

CHAPTER 12

I had sorted out my financial matters at Air Head-quarters New Delhi. I was now preparing to go and spend Christmas in Bombay. It took a great deal of mental preparation to return there. I would have to meet my relations without Percy. Knowing the mental, physical and emotional strain I would have to face, Noel decided to come to Delhi at the end of November to accompany us to Bombay.

The 22nd of November 1963 spelt disaster all over the world. The headlines of every newspaper announced the assassination of John Kennedy, President of the United States. If we thought that was bad, we came in for a greater shock! We read of an Indian Air Force helicopter that had met with a tragic accident at Poonch near Kashmir. All the occupants were killed outright. This included four or five Generals and Air Marshal Erlic Pinto. A massive dark cloud hung over Delhi that day.

I had never met Air Marshal Pinto. His wife Verna had come to pay her condolences to me in Chandigarh after Percy died. And now, it was my turn to pay my respects to her. As I entered her home, I recalled our conversation when she visited me at Chandigarh. As she took my hand in hers and said, "I am sorry," with such sincerity, I told her that I also said the same to many people who had suffered the loss of their loved ones. But I could never imagine the actual grief they were experiencing. It was only now that it had happened to me, could I realize the deep sorrow others had gone through.

I met Mrs. Pinto in her spacious house. She recognized me instantly even though we had only met for a brief time. Our eyes spoke volumes as I shook hands with her. I did not utter a word. There was a bond between us. A message flowed from my hand to hers. We shared something in common: grief over our loved ones stolen from us in the same tragic way.

There was a significant funeral service that evening. Freda my sister in law did not want me to attend, but I insisted on going. I stood there at the neat and well-kept graveyard in Delhi. Throngs of people came to pay their last respects to Air Marshal Pinto. The Last Post now sounded together with the 21 gun-salute. Four months earlier, when I heard this for Percy, I could not shed a tear. But now...now... the floodgates were open and I sobbed and sobbed. I cried my heart out. All the tears I withheld during Percy's funeral poured out for him now.

Friends around me were so upset that I came for the funeral as they saw me weeping so bitterly. But I was glad that all those pent-up feelings and emotions were released.

A few days later, it was time for yet another goodbye. We wished goodbye to Freda, Tony and to Delhi. We boarded the Frontier Mail, which would take us back to Bombay. As good as my brother Noel was, I could not help but think of the last trip we had taken just four months ago with Percy. What excitement there was as we traveled to our future together. And now, what did that future hold for me without my Percy?

My relations were really sympathetic when we arrived in Bombay. They welcomed us so lovingly and respected my feelings when I did not want to take part in the usual Christmas traditions at home. They did not do anything on an elaborate scale. The children received some toys, which they were only too happy to receive. I spent Christmas with my parents in Juhu and New Year with Percy's parents in Bandra. Going to church on both these occasions was so hard. I cried my heart out as I missed my Perce by my side.

Now that I was back on home ground, I had more time to think, time to ask questions. Time to ask a hundred thousand 'Whys.' There was one thing I became aware of. No matter how many times I asked "Why" I never got the answer. No matter how many times I asked God "Why God, why did You allow this to happen to me?" I would never receive a reply.

I realized, who was I to question my Maker? His ways are so much higher than ours and His thoughts are so much wiser. He knows what is best for each one of us. But I just wanted to know the reason. "Did You really take me at my word and give me someone to love and be the father of my children Lord and then take him away? Were You angry with me Lord, because I did not become a nun?" How many questions I asked, but not a single reply did I receive.

I did not understand the whys and wherefores. But when I look back, I can see God's hand. No matter what pain and sorrow I had been through, I know it was for a purpose. And I also know that all things yes **all things** work together for good to those who love the Lord and walk according to His purposes. Yes, I loved the Lord in my own way. God had to take me a long way, however, to nurture and train that love. He had to teach me, and is still teaching me to walk according to His purposes.

In my reflective periods, I thought of how devout and religious I had been. I was a very good practicing Roman Catholic. I had continued to follow all that I was taught by the nuns in the Convent in my formative years. I had great devotion to Mary and the Infant Jesus. I made numerous Novenas. I had kept the Nine First Fridays regularly. What about the promises that were attached to the keeping of these Nine First Fridays? The Sacred Heart of Jesus who had appeared to Saint Margaret Mary gave these promises we learned. I know Percy had also kept these First Fridays at some stage. Then what happened to the promise that he would receive the Sacraments at the time of his death? What happened on July 16th 1963? Was this promise fulfilled that night? There was no priest on the aircraft for Percy to make his confession.

So with all these doubts in my mind, I wrote to my former principal, Father Rehm from N.D.A. Khadakwasla. I asked him to explain this to me. He promptly replied to me. He said the promise stated that they would receive 'their' sacraments and not 'the' sacraments. He added Percy must have confessed his sins to Jesus and they were surely forgiven.

Unknowingly, this dear old priest (who is no more now) planted some vital seeds in my heart. If Percy confessed his sins to Jesus and had them forgiven, then why could I not do the same? What was the necessity of confessing our sins to a priest? It was just a thought. I did not know how to go about it, especially after being a practicing Catholic all my life. I continued going to Confession, as I had been brought up to do. But doubts and questions still kept flooding my mind.

After Christmas of 1963, I proceeded to Poona to be interviewed by Sister Susan, the Principal of St. Mary's before school reopened. I was brave enough to do this trip on my own. I left the children in Juhu with my parents and left by the afternoon train. Jessie and Peter Smith, friends of ours from the N.D.A. were now at Poona. They met me at the station and took me to the Rajendra Sinhji Institute (Army Mess) on Elphinstone Road where they were residing. This was the first time we were meeting after Percy's death, so there was much to share.

The next morning, Jessie came with me to St. Mary's to give me Dutch courage. As we entered the gates, I was really surprised at the first glimpse of this school. I had always associated schools with huge, massive structures. But I saw something that resembled sheds! I asked Jessie what they were, and she informed me they were classrooms! The buildings were all spread out ... a few classrooms here and a few classrooms there. In spite of that, the homely atmosphere struck me, as I walked through the garden, down the corridor and into the Principal's office. We took to each other instantly. I could not wait to begin teaching there.

I returned to Bombay that evening to find Cheryl down with a nasty attack of measles. It was evident that Robin and Patty would follow likewise. It was sad, as they would be left behind and school was to reopen shortly. I had to go and set up home in Poona. I had applied to the Sub Area Commander requesting if I could have temporary accommodation on compassionate grounds. He kindly agreed that I could have two rooms in the R.S.I. the same Mess where Jessie and Pete were staying. I was allowed to stay there for three months only and I would have to pay 'market rent.'

'Beggars can't be choosers' and so I agreed. It did take quite a bit of adjusting to settle in the R.S.I. Quarters. I thought of the spacious house we had left in Chandigarh. Now we had to be content with two tiny rooms. Our trunks were stacked one above the other. I unpacked the bare necessities.

My Dad came along with me and helped me to set up home. It was formerly a block of bachelor officers' quarters. Now it had been converted into married accommodation. We had two rooms with two toilets attached. We converted one toilet into a kitchen.

These toilets were a scream! Suddenly, without any warning, the flush would work automatically and we would jump up with a fright. One would not think water was a problem with a flush like that, but it was. It was such a boon having Dad with me. I would not have managed without him. Every morning, he would carry our buckets to the backyard and collect our daily supply of water.

While Dad was with me, Noel and Sybil were at home in Juhu with Mum and the children. My elder sister June was posted at Cuttack with her husband Tony and their three daughters.

It was fortunate that my accommodation was in the heart of town. We could just walk down to Kayani Bakery for our daily supply of fresh bread; to say nothing of the famous Shrewsbury biscuits! Or even drop in at Mangal Vihar for a quick dosa or vada. Dad used to drive me to school and back.

As soon as the children had recovered from their measles, Mum and Sybil brought them to Poona. Dad returned to Bombay. Mum decided to stay with me for some time, till I was more settled. She was concerned about Robin and Patty at home, while I took Cheryl to school. Fortunately, we contacted Lakshmi, our old servant, who had worked with us in Khadakwasla, when Robin was a baby. She was only too happy to come back and work with us.

Talking of Lakshmi, she was quite a character! When she first came for employment, she told us she could not cook, neither could she speak nor understand English. Day after day, I would look up the recipe books and give her instructions in my broken

Hindi. Lakshmi managed to serve us our daily meals. One day, I heard all the old English songs being sung with gusto, and for sure I knew it was not Cheryl singing. When I opened the door there was Lakshmi entertaining Robin and Cheryl singing 'I'm forever blowing bubbles,' and 'Show me the way to go home' and a few other old favorites.

If that floored me, she just took the cake when on Easter Sunday she told me she would manage the lunch on her own. Of course I was nervous, as we had invited a friend over. There was no need to fear as Lakshmi had the table spread with a lavish meal. She was such an excellent cook; besides being an actress! She had fooled me all along and must have been having a good chuckle each day as I explained to her how to cook and what to cook etc. She could have got away with all the Oscars available! It was good having Lakshmi with us again.

The children were thrilled with their new home. It made no difference to them whether it was big or small, as long as we were together. We had a park near our rooms. They enjoyed themselves playing on the swings, slides and merry go round. Instead of staying in the R.S.I. for three months, we stayed there for three years by God's grace. During this time my dream home was being built in St. Patrick's Town.

CHAPTER 13

It was a good experience for me, teaching in St. Mary's School under the loving and able guidance of Lily Hyams, the Headmistress. The classes were small. We had a maximum of twenty five to thirty children in each class. We were thus able to give individual attention to each child. At first I was appointed to teach in Std.I. After a few months, when one of the teachers left to get married, I was promoted to Std. II. This classroom was in one of the sheds!

St. Mary's or rather Lily, was very particular about us filling our classrooms with charts. We had to display our Handwork and Progress Charts. It was worth the effort, because all the classrooms looked so gay and inviting. I would be so frustrated each morning as I entered my shed! There were visitors in my class before I could even enter. The crows used to come in and peck at my charts. We tried setting booby traps to keep them away, but they still entered.

The teachers in the Prep School were very kind and helpful. It was an extremely homely atmosphere. I came to know them better as we chatted and joked over lunch. Most often I would take part in the conversation with a smile plastered on my face. Actually, I went around with a number of masks. The teachers thought I was very brave and bold. I went around with this brave exterior for the benefit of the world. It was just to cover up that deep, deep hurt and loneliness within.

Once school was over and I would go home, I would long for Percy. It was so difficult to think of life without him. Would he ever come back? Could he? I needed someone to share my innermost feelings with...someone to rely on ... someone to love. I had depended on Percy for every detail; and now overnight, it was all my responsibility.

I loved my children immensely but they were too young. I could not talk to them and share the things that were on my heart. As much as I wanted to go out and see a film now and then, I refrained from doing so. I knew watching a romance would cause the pain in my heart to increase all the more. I longed for Percy. He was such a gentle lover and he taught me all there was to know of love.

"Percy, Percy, why did you leave me my darling? I want you. I need you my Perce." It was so difficult to think of life without Percy. I would cry my heart out at times, but I would try to conceal this from the children.

On one occasion, however, Robin my dear son came in and caught me sobbing on my bed. "Why are you crying Mama? You want Daddy?" I just drew him towards me and hugged him. "Yes my son, I want Daddy." And my darling three-year-old son, the only man in our family, strutted off promptly and got a photograph of his Dad from the next room. He put it in my hand and said, "Take Mama . . .here is Daddy. Now don't cry anymore, okay?" Mission accomplished, he went to join the others in the park. What did my little innocent son know? He must have thought that a picture of a person could make up for his presence.

Home and school, school and home. Life went on like this for months. I soon felt happier in St. Mary's and part of my mischievous self-surfaced. I was the ringleader of many practical jokes among the staff members. I typed letters to two teachers thanking them for their services and serving them with notice. Once they received the letter through the peon and I saw them looking so upset, I was the first to console them with a straight and innocent face.

On April Fool's Day, I added Epsom salts in the teapot at break time. Only two other teachers, Lily and Phyllis were aware of this. We pretended to sip our tea and complained of the peculiar taste. As soon as the others left grumbling at the horrible tea we were served that day, I pulled out my flask and the three of us shared the most delicious coffee I had brought from home. But the joke had ill effects that night. Poor dear Mrs. Oliver had a very bad night. She thought she was going to have a heart attack. When it came to light and we confessed our prank, we heard that she was allergic to Epsom salts! How dreadful! With solemn faces, we resolved not to play any more jokes. But the following year when April Fool's Day arrived, there was I at it again.

This time I did not confine my pranks to St. Mary's. I went to the next compound and met Mr.Lunn, Principal of Bishop's School. He was a good sport and game to join the fun. I asked him for a sheet of paper with his school's letterhead. I shared my plan with him and he willingly agreed. I went across to our school office and asked the secretary to type a letter to Aloo, one of the teachers. She was informed that her son who was in the Senior Cambridge Class at Bishop's was not doing very well. The Principal desired to meet her that evening, to discuss her son's progress. The letter was duly signed. The school peon went to her class and delivered it to her.

That evening Aloo happened to be on Bus Duty. Very innocently, I passed through the hall and observed her separating the children into their different bus groups. She called me aside with tears in her eyes, and showed me the letter. I had to use all my self-control not to spoil the joke at the last minute. I told her not to take it to heart but to go across and see what Mr. Lunn had to say. I even offered to do her duty while she went across for her appointment at four o'clock. The other teachers, who were aware of the joke, were watching from Lily's office, suppressing their laughter.

If Aloo had just walked straight into Mr. Lunn's office, he would have told her it was a big joke. But no! She was not going to face the Principal alone. She sent for her son and marched him into the office ahead of her. She gave him a good dressing down. Now poor Mr. Lunn could not possibly reveal that it was a joke. He had to tell Yazad to pull up his socks and work real hard. Oh dear! These jokes were getting from bad to worse. I really had to call it a day!

Robin and Patricia joined St. Mary's. Now we all went to the same school together. At last, it seemed like we had turned the painful corner of tears and goodbyes. But how many painful corners did I have to turn to get to the Nursery God had told me to start?

CHAPTER 14

Percy had given me my first driving lessons, but now I felt I would never have the confidence to drive on my own. One fine day, however, Percy's brother Cedric landed at St. Mary's with 'Black Beauty'. Promptly, he handed me the keys and said, "Come on drive." I replied that I could not possibly do so. I made a hundred excuses but to no avail. Cedric said, "Come on just try. It will all come back."

When Percy was by my side while I was driving, if I saw two cycles or a bullock cart ahead of me, I would scream for help and try to brake. Like many lady drivers or rather, like many beginners, instead of pressing the brake I would get confused and press the accelerator. When corrected gently by Percy, I would get annoyed and say, "then you drive, I am not going to drive anymore."

I knew Percy was always there to take over, but now, I could not play the same tricks with anyone else, not even his brother. So with Cedric's persuasion, I got into the driver's seat and was I amazed! It all came back. Put the gear in neutral, switch on. I felt good. I felt like a veteran. I realized this was the only way. I just had to get going on my own. I knew this would not come easily. It would mean daily practice. If I did not succeed, I would have to sell the car. So, with real determination and effort on my part, I headed for the Race Course every evening. I took my mosquito poles along with me and planted them on the field to practice reversing in order to prepare for my driving test.

Soon I had my Learner's license ready and my 'L' plate fixed. It was great driving around. My confidence increased in driving as in other things. Except while parking on Main Street...the reversing made me nervous.

At last on Maundy Thursday in April 1964, I went for my driving test in fear and trepidation. The inspector sat by my side and made me go for a short drive. That seemed quite simple. Then came what I feared... the reversing. It started well, but then, I felt the gears get very stiff. Just as I was coming to the end of the test, I closed my eyes and said, "Percy, why can't you help me out of this my darling?" Believe it or not, with closed eyes I got through the last bit without dropping the poles! It was unbelievable but true. I certainly do not recommend this to anyone! It was a real miracle how I got through without dropping a pole. Never again would I attempt to close my eyes and reverse.

The inspector took what seemed like an age to come to me with his verdict. I could feel my heart pounding as I saw him approaching. When he told me I had passed the test, I just could not believe it.

I was overjoyed. I went home full of jubilation. My Mum was staying with me at that time. I said to her, "Come on Mum, get dressed. Let's go to church." "Who will take us?" she asked. Like a smart cockatoo I replied, "What a question, mother dear; none other than yours truly. I have got my license today and I am no longer a learner."

She came with me, but I think she must have had her heart in her mouth. It took quite some time for her to sit down at ease by my side. She could not believe this daughter of hers would ever have the confidence to drive on these busy roads. Since I was alone, I had to gain confidence in many more things just as I did in driving.

I was mother and father to my children. Either I had to learn to do things myself or always be dependant on others to help us for everything. The children were thrilled that their Mama could drive them about in 'Black Beauty'. It was a real treat for them. At the least excuse, we would jump into the car and go for a picnic. Any outing was called a picnic. If they made a fuss to eat their food, I would say, "Come on for a picnic" and each of them with their bowls in their hands would pile into the car.

Invariably, I would drive to the Race Course or to Empress Gardens. The different surroundings would improve their appetites and soon their bowls would be empty. Whenever possible, I would take them for long drives and soon my confidence increased. The more I attempted to do things for myself, the more my self-confidence grew.

My days seemed to be getting fuller. I was busy with more and more activities. The contractor, together with the priest who sold us the plot, came to draw the plans for my house at St. Patrick's Town. To me, this place was only a name in an address. I had to drive there to see the exact location. I was told it was just opposite the Army School of Physical Training, better known as A.S.P.T. This was at the foot of Ramtekdi Hill. (It was a real coincidence: our home was going to be built opposite Percy's and my Blueberry Hill.)

In those days, it seemed quite a distance from town. We had to drive past the Race Course, then through the busy, narrow road of Bhairoba Nalla. On both sides of the road we passed cemeteries. To the right we spotted the A.S.P.T. but where was St. Patrick's Town? We looked on the opposite side and all we could see were thorny bushes. A lone stable stood in the midst of all this thorny overgrowth. Was *this* St. Patrick's Town? I never ever imagined this Co-operative Housing Society would ever come into existence.

All the same I proceeded with my plans. I reminded the contractor that we had to build my house in such a way as to accommodate my Nursery (the one I was told to have.)

I made it clear to him that all I had was Percy's life insurance of Rs. 25,000/ - We would **have** to build the house in that amount. (In those days, the Air Force gave no insurance and extra benefits to widows as they do now.) However, the priest had given me his word he would get me a loan from Germany. So plans were made and remade. On one hand we were working on the plans and on the other hand, I would take the children for a drive now and then to see if there was any hope and chance of St. Patrick's Town materializing.

It honestly seemed like a dream. On one of our drives, as we beheld this vast expanse of thorny growth, we seemed to see something new! What was that? Our eyes fell on a large heap of stones. I squealed with delight. Imagine getting excited over a heap of stones! But it was new! Something was added to the view we were so used to seeing each time we drove by. The children added to the squeals. The excitement was contagious! There was hope that something was going to happen at last.

A short time later, plots were divided and I was allotted '79.' It was anyone's guess where '79' was. There were no roads or pathways in so-called St. Patrick's Town in those days. After walking and walking through the thorny growth and carrying away thorns on our clothes, at last we found it! On a little white stone we found written '79.'

A few days later we had the plot blessed and the building committed to God. The foundation was laid and the dream house started taking shape. The dealers needed payment and would come to me and I in turn would send them to the priest. He would send them back to me. I wondered what was going on. Was this some kind of game? I signed cheques and more cheques...till I could sign no more. I had nothing left and the house was not complete. What could I do? I went to the priest and asked if the loan had come through. I was more than shocked, when for no reason at all, he just wiped his hands off the project completely.

Gone were the promises of the loan from Germany. I asked him to recall his letters and his promises. Shocking as it may seem but this priest went back on his word. I asked him how could he ever do such a thing. I could not believe this could be done by anyone to a widow and least of all by a priest! So, there was I left to face this battle alone. It was too much to bear. The building was coming up and the funds had gone down. Till there was nothing . . . absolutely nothing left in the bank.

CHAPTER 15

Now that I had no money would my house ever be complete? I turned to some members of my family for help, but drew a blank. If I knew this was going to happen, I would have definitely planned a much smaller house. But there was no need to. I was promised a loan and was fully assured that the plan would fit my budget.

At last, after running around in circles, some friends helped me to procure a loan from the Bank of Maharashtra. I had to pay quite a heavy interest on the loan, but I had no choice. With all these obstacles, it seemed impossible, but eventually, the house came up and what is more, was even completed.

On November 19th 1966, the house was blessed. I chose this day, as it was Percy's birthday. I invited my friends and we had a lovely house-warming party. Our makeshift table was one of the doors raised on bricks. It was laden with eats contributed by my friends. My children and I were thrilled because soon we would shift into our own house. But could I really call it our own? No! Not till I paid all my loans.

I chose to shift into our home on the 26th January 1967, as it was a public holiday. I had asked for an army truck on payment. Just as we were loading our luggage, who should arrive but Cedric and one of his nephews. Without being aware of it, they came just in time to help us. They were more than welcome. I needed that extra help.

After unloading our belongings from the truck, I tried to cook our first meal at '79' only to find there was no water and no electricity. Fortunately, we had collected water from the tap outside and lit some candles. It surely was a sad welcome!

We were among the pioneers of St. Patrick's Town. Water was scarce. You had to see it to believe it was there. I can still recall those days. I would call out, "Wake up children, wake up. It's time to get ready for school." All I would get in response would be yawns and sleepy eyes peering at me. It was quite a feat getting my three children up and ready for school. There would be such a scramble to the toilet.

Suddenly, I would hear a yell, "Mamaaaaaa, there's no water again today." This is what it was like day after day. Quite often we would ration ourselves to just one mug of water to wash our faces! We really had to be satisfied with a cat's lick.

After breakfast I would call "Come on babes, collect the water bottles and put them in the car."

"Why Mama, are we going for a picnic?" they would ask longingly.

"No darlings, no chance of a picnic. We are going to school."

"Then why are we taking our bottles to school Mama?"

Imagine taking our bottles to school! The reason being- I used to fill them with drinking water there. While we were away at school, our servant would take our clothes and wash them at the canal close by. On weekends, we would visit a friend's place to have a real good bath and scrub! These are all memories of the past. When we think back we cannot believe we survived but we did! And we enjoyed every moment of it!

It was fun, but we could not go on living like this forever. So we had a pit dug at the back and had a water tank fitted in. Whenever we would get water from the mains, it would flow into this tank. At times, it was merely a trickle. But 'every drop fills an ocean.' So eventually, the tank also got filled.

We bought an electric pump to send the water from the tank below to the tank on our terrace. For the first time in over two years, we could open our taps and see running water. What joy!

When we shifted into St. Patrick's Town, there were just about three or four houses dotting this vast bare landscape. After some time, however, due to seed dispersal, custard apple and guava trees grew wild, attracting flocks of pretty green parrots.

We could see the railway lines clearly from our house and watch the trains go by. We had no road lights at all and as for the roads, they were just dusty pathways. If we needed anything, there was no such thing as going across to the now nearby Poona Cheap Stores. It did not exist! We had to go all the way to town. Fortunately, I had to drive to school daily, so I would jot down what was needed on my shopping list and collect the items on my way home.

Saturday, however, was 'Market Day.' The children would be thrilled with any outing. Meat, vegetables, fruit, were the main items on the list. They would get so excited helping me to empty all our purchases into the dickey. No trip to the market was complete without delicious market ice cream. Licking our cones and singing happily, we would return home with our weekly purchases.

For the first time since Percy's death, the children and I were experiencing the joy of our very own home...Then one day, terror struck!

CHAPTER 16

It was a quiet still night, as I was relaxing in my bed, reading. The children were in the sitting room with my sister Sybil. Then suddenly, I heard a loud C-R-A-S-H. It did not take me long to realize that the crash I heard was the smash of the window pane near my bed. But HOW did it happen? WHY did it happen? WHO did it? All these questions went fleeting through my mind. My heart was pounding in fear. The children and Sybil, were they safe?

With fear and dread in my heart, but with a bold front, I went to the sitting room to see what the children were doing. To my surprise, they had not heard a thing. Patty was playing the piano; Cheryl was painting and Robin completing his homework. Sybil was putting last minute touches to one of her pieces of Art and Craft. I signaled to Sybil quietly and led her to the bedroom. I pointed to the window but could not say much. Both of us were terrified. But while the children kept on with their activities in the sitting room, we -- like a couple of detectives, tried to get to the bottom of this mystery.

With teeth chattering and knees knocking, we drew the curtains so that the culprits would not be able to see us from outside, in case they were still there. We found splinters from the pane on my bed. By the way the window was hit, we knew it was no mistake. It was not that somebody had thrown a stone from the road by accident. It was evident that the person had come up to the neighbor's fence and taken a deliberate and direct shot at the window.

But WHY? I began to examine my conscience. Who were my enemies? I could not dream of any. I just put these thoughts aside as Sybil and I cleared all traces of the splintered glass from my bed. I drew the curtains across, so that there would be no visible traces of what had happened when the children came to bed. I did not want them to be alarmed and spend a fearful night. God kept filling me with such a generous portion of strength and courage externally, but I was dying a hundred deaths within.

I summoned the children to bed and acted as if nothing had happened. "Come on children, put away your books and get ready to sleep." After they undressed, we got ready to pray as we did every night. With childlike innocence they repeated the prayers I had taught them. They asked Jesus to take care of us as we slept. I kissed each of them goodnight and tucked them in their beds.

But was it a good night for me? Far from it! I was so scared. My fear took such a hold of me. I could not lie down quietly. I kept pacing to and from the toilet, getting violently sick. It was a nightmarish night. If only I could sleep! I could hear each hour chime in the distance. And as I paced to and fro, getting sick, my imagination ran riot, wondering who this person could be. What were his intentions? If he meant business, he could even stone our car, when we went to school daily. I was petrified. How I longed for Percy. Why oh why did you leave me my Perce? What am I going to do? How will I face these many morrows alone without you?

It was dreadful if things like this were going to happen. Just the three small children, Sybil and myself at home! Should I get a tenant? It would surely be good to have a man on the premises. Anyway there was no time to think of the future. Sybil and I kept wondering who this person could be. I then recalled that on a Sunday morning, a few weeks ago, just as we were getting ready to leave for church, an old woman came begging. She was dressed very well and even had a gold chain round her neck. I did not see why she should beg for money. Since she was persisting, and it was getting late for us to go to church, I went into the house and got some bread for her. She took it instantly and flung it on the ground. Cursing me in all the foul language possible, she said, "Do you think I have waited all this time for this? You wait and see what I will do to you...just wait and see." She mumbled this as she kept wagging her bony finger at me. The old witch continued cursing me. She used to live in the Gut Factory on the road behind us. Could **she** have instigated someone to do this in revenge?

That evening, we returned from school still scared out of our wits, not knowing what to expect next. By this time, it was no longer a secret from the children. They found me acting strange. I presume they might have overheard Sybil and myself discussing our plan of action. We did not make it sound too serious to them. We mentioned some bad people were passing on the road and had thrown a stone, which had smashed our windowpane. We told them we wanted to try and catch these horrid people. We continued drawing our curtains so that nobody could look inside our house. It was very frightening, sitting and waiting for something to happen . . .

Something **did** happen, sooner than we had expected. The doorbell rang, louder and shriller than ever. It sent shivers down my spine. With a prayer in my heart, I went to the door. The children and Sybil followed close behind as my bodyguards. Two men stood there. Immediately, I recognized them from the Gut Factory quarters, the same place where that old woman had come from.

These fellows had the nerve to ask me if I had a room for rent. I did not have any tenants just then, but on the spur of the moment, I said that my room was rented to a police officer who was out of station but was returning that evening. I felt quite justified telling them this fiction. What I had surmised had been confirmed. I put two and two together and knew the old woman must have sent them.

As soon as they left, we immediately drove to the P.T. School opposite our colony. I explained to the Commandant what had happened. He kindly appointed two guards to watch over our house every night. They would report for duty at sunset, and leave early the next morning. A week went by and all seemed safe and peaceful. So we decided to go and visit a friend. When we returned, we saw a crowd at our gate.

Now WHAT? As we approached '79,' we were told that the windows of the other bedroom had been smashed. Evidently, the culprits had observed when the sentries came on duty and might have seen us going out. So, before the guards or we could arrive, they got into action. Our very lives were in danger. Four large windows smashed in broad daylight! What next?

I was certain those two men who had come and asked for our room on rent, must have done it. And I sincerely believed they were connected with that old woman. The next morning, I went to the Commissioner of Police with the Commandant of the A.S.P.T. I lodged a complaint and also shared my suspicion. I believe they caught these suspects and threatened them severely at the Police Station, because after this, life seemed normal and peaceful again. I carried on with boldness outside but I must admit I still had absolute dread and fear within. This episode was enough to scare me. I had no idea what to expect next. It was terrible to live in fear. "Fear is not of the Lord," is written in the Bible. But I had never read the Bible in those days. It took us some time to get over these fears.

Peace reigned over our house. The Commandant from the A.S.P.T. would come over to enquire if everything was fine. When things seemed to have settled down and there was no more recurrence of stone throwing, the guards were taken off their special duty at '79.' But little did we know that other dangers lay just a stone's throw away.

CHAPTER 17

I n January 1969, we decided as a family, to venture out in our famous 'Black Beauty' to Ahmednagar and from there to visit the Ajanta and Ellora Caves. I felt we needed a break. Life had gone on in the same cycle. School, tuitions, housework, children's home-work and then the long, lonely hours of the nights I had to face alone. How was I to fill these lonely hours? There was reading, but books did not fill that void and emptiness in my life. I would read till the early hours of the morning. Not being able to sleep, I would resort to a sleeping pill just to get a few hours of sleep before the next day's routine. And that is how life continued for a long, long time.

But now, the Ajanta trip was something to look forward to. My friend Mitzi a nurse in the Military Hospital in Poona, had taken a few days leave and decided to join us. The children, Sybil and our servant, piled into the back while Mitzi and I sat in front. The dickey was filled with our bedding and clothes. Sybil was in charge of the food and water for the way. Just before I reversed the car out of the driveway, we prayed and committed the trip into God's hands. We asked Him to be with us, to keep us safe and let us have a wonderful trip. We always made it a practice to pray and ask God to be with us, whether I took the children for a short drive or a long one.

I locked the gate and asked God to keep our home safe while we were away. Once I got behind the wheel, I said each one had to take it in turns to start a song and we would all join in. What fun we had! We sang one song after another. It could not have been a happier day. As we left the busy roads of Poona behind, the road seemed to be just for us. There was only the odd bus or truck for quite a stretch. Seeing the roads so clear, I drove the car to the side of the road and exchanged places with Mitzi. She continued to drive, while I conducted the choir! Songs, smiles, laughter! Everything was fine for miles.

There was a bus ahead of us. As much as we wanted to overtake it, we were unable to do so, as the driver kept hogging the road. I know my last words to Mitzi were, "Be careful of the bus." I do not recall why I said it. Neither do I recall anything that happened immediately after that. My head hit the windscreen and I had lost my memory for quite a while. It was only later that I came to know what had happened.

The bus driver had suddenly swerved right to enter the bus depot without giving any signal or slowing down. To avoid colliding with the bus, Mitzi had swerved to the right and the car crashed into the wall of the bus station. I had no idea what had happened to the car nor was I aware that we were taken in a State Transport bus to a nearby dispensary for first aid. Everything was a blank. I kept pacing the floor, saying things I was not aware of. My children thought I had gone round the bend. They were not sure whether to laugh or cry as they kept observing me. They disclosed all this to me later.

Mitzi was given local anaesthesia and the doctor sutured both her knees. After attending to her, he then came to me and jerked my head to see if I needed stitches and suddenly... I seemed to come back to my senses with that jerk. I wondered what we were doing and how we had landed in this place. I told Sybil to take me to the car, as I was ready to drive them home.

They stared at me aghast. It was only when I reached the site of the accident that I realized why they had looked at me as they did. The right side of the car was completely smashed. I knew I had to work overtime then. I do not know where and how I got the strength and ability to do all I did...especially in that frame of mind. All I can say now, that it was God's loving hand leading and guiding me with every detail.

I phoned my Insurance Agent informing him of the accident. I then phoned the Commandant of the Signals Unit, whose daughter was in my class. I asked him to please send us a vehicle to tow my car back to Poona. I also requested him to phone the Military Hospital and inform the Matron about our accident and request her to please keep a room ready for us. I was amazed that I could have possibly thought of these numerous details on my own in that condition. Surely, it was divine guidance by our Heavenly Father.

It was a nightmarish drive back to Poona after we finished all the formalities with the police. Fortunately, we had taken our bedding with us, so we placed it for Mitzi to lie on, as she was in excruciating pain. By this time, my head had also started throbbing with great intensity. Every now and then, I wondered if the towed car would bang into the truck and cause further damage. Whereas we had taken one and a half hour to reach Sirur the site of our accident, we took over five hours to return. It was a most painful trip in more sense than one. We headed straight for the M.I.Room and reported there. We were directed to our room, which had been prepared for us. Mitzi and I were admitted in the hospital, while Sybil and the children spent the night in the Matron's room.

There was much to thank God for that day. Surely, His hand was on each of us. I recalled committing our trip into His hands that morning. We had prayed and asked Him to be with us. In spite of what we went through, I thanked God for His nearness and presence. He certainly has not said we will be exempt from troubles but He has promised to be with us as we go through these troubles. In the book of Isaiah, Ch.43: 2-3, He said, *"When you pass through deep waters I will be with you. Your troubles will not overwhelm you. When you pass through fire, you will not be burnt. The hard trials that come will not hurt you. For I am the Lord your God, the Holy God of Israel who saves you."* And so He did. He saved us from something that could have been much worse.

I could not stop thanking God. With all the pain and discomfort I was going through, I praised God there were no bones broken, no brain damage. I praised God that I did not die outright. What would have happened to my children if they were left alone? God surely had His hand on us and protected us from the worst.

I thanked Him for the divine guidance and strength He gave me to contact the correct people. I know that on my own, I would never have dreamt of doing all I had done that afternoon. *"I will never leave you nor forsake you."* (Hebrews 13:5.) Oh what a great great God! I begged His forgiveness for the times I had forsaken Him. Yet He is so loving...so forgiving... so true to His Word. With a heart overflowing with praise and thanksgiving to God, I managed to have snatches of sleep that night with the painkillers they had given me.

We were in hospital for nearly a month. Mitzi could not walk. Her knees were stiff and painful. Big bruises appeared round my eyes and head. The top of my head was absolutely numb. Various tests were carried out daily to see if there was any internal damage. I was advised complete rest. Even after I was discharged from the hospital, I could not return to school for quite a while. My head used to reel in pain and I would get giddy spells. I stayed at home for some time to recover. But that period also passed and I finally went back to school.

St. Patrick's feast is celebrated on the 17th of March. As loyal citizens of St. Patrick's Town, we were going to celebrate this feast by having a get-together that evening. My mother and Noel my brother had come to spend the weekend with us and were returning to Bombay that day. I told the children and Sybil to get dressed and ready for the party, while I drove Mum and Noel to the station. I promised to be back soon.

At the station I got into the compartment and was chatting with them. Suddenly, before I was aware of it, the train started. I was in a panic. I could have gone to Kirkee the next station, and returned in a rickshaw to collect the car. But no! Panic gripped me. All kinds of thoughts flashed through my mind. Should I jump out of the train? The car was parked outside ...the children were waiting to go for the party... and so I jumped! I landed on my knees at the edge of the platform.

Again, God's hand was on me in a mighty way. Thankfully, I fell at the edge of the platform and not between the platform and the train, or I would have been under the wheels. The train sped by, unaware of the one soul who had fallen out, crouched there in pain. Outwardly I was the picture of courage as always, but inside, I was completely shattered. Both my knees had nasty wounds. I limped to a tap on the platform and washed my wounds. I brazenly walked out of the station and stepped into my car. It was only when I sat in the car that I realized ...I had SOMEONE to thank. I said "Thank you God for saving me." What if I had gone under the train? Just the thought of it sent a shudder down my spine. There would have been nobody to tell the story to Sybil and my children waiting at home for me.

"Thank you Lord, thank you," I could not stop thanking Him after that. Instead of driving to the closest hospital at Poona, I drove all the way to the Military Hospital at Kirkee, as Mitzi was working there. Once I reached her room, the bold exterior crumbled, the mask came down and I cried and cried. "What's happened Marge?" she asked.

"I could have died just now," I replied.

"But what happened? Try and be calm and tell me."

"I jumped out of the train Mitzi. I did not know how to jump."

She could not discern what I was trying to say as I was crying so much. She made me sit down and gave me a hot drink. It was then that she saw my knees. I explained to her how I jumped out of the train after it started.

"I thought it was the best thing to do," I wailed, "but it could have been the end."

Mitzi cleaned my wounds with disinfectant and gave me an anti-tetanus injection. "Mitzi, the children and Sybil are waiting for me. They are dressed and ready to go for the party this evening," I told her. I was in no state to drive back and definitely could not dream of going to the party. Mitzi appointed one of the nurses to stay with me, while she went to '79' to inform Sybil and the children what had happened. When they heard the scooter, they rushed to the gate, "Mummy is not here. We do not know where she is. She told us to get dressed for the party and she would come back soon from the station." They all kept talking to her together. She had to calm them down and then gently and tactfully, broke the news to them.

Fear was written all over their faces but she assured them all was well. She told them I was very shaken by what had happened, but I would definitely come home the following morning. Much against their will, they proceeded to the party with Sybil. They could not enjoy it much, as they wondered about me and were filled with fear.

After a restless night, I managed to drive home the next morning, in time to take them to school. All the while I was thinking, "Why did He save me?" He had now saved me from two accidents in quick succession. Surely, it must be for a purpose. But what could it be? I could not guess.

In October 1969 it happened again! I was riding pillion on a friend's scooter. The tyre pressure was low and before we reached a petrol pump to have it filled...THUD! I was down on the road. I heard the screech of brakes behind me. The driver of a large truck had managed to jam his brakes in time.

This was a bit too much for one year. January, March, October. I had to sit down and sort things out in my mind. WHY, WHY had I been saved like this? Would I ever know why God saved me from these near fatal accidents? Not once, not twice but three times in the same year! Should I write a book about all this?? But how would I do it?

I carried on teaching at St. Mary's School but I felt the need to obey the divine instructions I had received at Chandigarh to build a house and have a Nursery. The house I had built and even paid for it completely by now. My father in law stepped in and helped me by completing the payment to the contractor. I was most grateful to him for this generous gesture on his part.

But what about the Nursery? Was it possible? I did not have the means but the more I thought of it, the more I knew I must step out in faith. What would I do for furniture? Packing cases could be the answer!

I decided to ask the leading stores in Poona if I could buy some large cases from them. I voiced these thoughts to Bashie, a good friend of mine from the Air Force. She in turn went to Mrs. Latif, who was the Station Commander's wife. I had never met her before, but I had heard from many people that she was a very kind and understanding lady. Bashie told Mrs. Latif that I was a widow with three small children and found it extremely difficult to make ends meet. She mentioned to her that I wanted to better my prospects by starting a Nursery School.

"Wouldn't it be good if we could help her?" asked Bashie. "She was one of us a short time ago and now she is a struggling widow. Who knows? Any of us could be in the same plight as her one day," she added.

Mrs. Latif needed no more prompting. She organized a fete and collected money to enable me to start my Nursery. Moreover, she sent a truck, not with packing cases as I had requested, but with large desks and benches attached. I was more than grateful to her and to Bashie for this generous help. My Dad came from Bombay with a carpenter. Under his supervision, we soon had the benches cut down to size. They were transformed into little tables and chairs. Sybil and I got down to painting them in pastel shades. At last my dream began to take shape

CHAPTER 18

It was on the 4th of January 1970, that a few people gathered together at "Happy Hours," for that is what I decided to name my Nursery. The Bishop of Poona came to dedicate it to Almighty God. Sybil my sister, who had completed her Teachers' Training at St.Mary's College, agreed to teach in the Nursery for a year till it was established. School commenced on the 7th January with seven children. It was a beginning!

In 1971, I left St.Mary's School after spending seven wonderful and beneficial years there, and came to enjoy happy hours at "Happy Hours." By now we had twenty children aged between two and a half and five years. Word had spread. What a difference it made working on home ground. No more rushing to school daily. It was so convenient teaching at home, and so rewarding. School hours were from nine o'clock till noon. I could fit in my housework in a leisurely manner.

Though I enjoyed my Nursery, I still wondered WHY I was told by God to have it. Perhaps one day,

I would know the reason. Different people were brought into my life now. Among them, were a very devout Scottish couple, Rev. John McLeod and his wife Sheila. He was the pastor of St. Mary's Anglican Church in Poona. This couple played a very important role in our lives. They knew how to put into practice what they believed and preached.

They showed Christian love to all whom they came in contact with. They never preached 'at us,' but their lives spoke volumes. I had taught their daughter at St.Mary's, but at that time, I did not come into close contact with them. But now that I had started my Nursery, the McLeods requested me to admit their two little sons Rory and Hamish. It was an honor that they chose my Nursery, as they had to drive quite a distance to and fro. Hamish was so young. He used to attend school armed with a change of nappies and his plastic pants!

Having to meet the McLeods daily brought us closer to each other. I remember the first time Sheila asked me to attend a Pentecostal meeting. My first response was to decline. It was because of my ignorance, perhaps. I was scared of speaking in tongues. I thought it would just happen all of a sudden and I would not be able to control myself. So I said, "No thanks, Sheila, I would rather not come with you. I am scared I may start speaking in tongues." She did not pursue the matter.

One day, however, Sheila asked me if I would like to read a book. Who can say 'no' to that? I used to read myself to sleep. But this was quite a different book compared to those I usually read!

She gave me "The Cross and the Switchblade" by David Wilkerson. The book gripped my heart. I realized that the Holy Spirit is alive. Alive and active! I read snatches of the book to the children. I could not believe the way that He could work in peoples' lives. The first seeds, no doubt, were being sown from that book in my heart.

This was the first time I read about 'laying fleeces' before the Lord. In the book of Judges chapter 6, we read of how Gideon placed a fleece before God. He asked God for a sign. He put wool on the ground where they threshed wheat. He told God if there was dew on the wool in the morning he would know that God would use him to rescue Israel. And that is exactly what happened the next morning. He squeezed the wool and wrung enough water to fill a bowl with it.

The next day Gideon asked God to keep the wool dry and make the ground wet and lo and behold! that is exactly how he found it. It was not putting God to the test, but Gideon wanted to know God's will through a definite sign. After reading this, I suddenly found myself 'laying fleeces' before the Lord.

For instance, at that time, I wanted to know if it was God's will for me to continue giving piano tuitions. I said, "Lord, if You want me to continue with these tuitions, show me through my pupils' results." And the results were really good, so I knew that it was God's will for me to continue. In big things or small, I always wanted to know God's will in my life.

After reading "The Cross and the Switchblade" I hungered for more good books to read. Gradually all those former books of mine were cleared from the shelf near my bed. Soon I started reading good and wholesome Christian literature. What a difference it made to my life.

It was about this time that a friend of ours had been operated. Sheila said, " Let us pray for her." I replied I had done so already.

"No," she said, "let us go to the hospital and pray for her."

So we went along with yet another friend. At the hospital, after exchanging a few pleasantries, Sheila was ready to pray. She did not start the mechanical prayers, which I was accustomed to but started **talking** to Jesus, as if He were right there in our midst. The other lady followed suit, and then there was an uncanny silence as they waited for me to pray. Try as I would, nothing would emerge from my mouth. I could feel my face getting flushed. I tried to open my mouth but not a sound!

They continued praying and talking to God. I wondered why I could not do the same. At last, I plucked up courage and a few words spluttered out. My face was as red as a beetroot. I realized how difficult it is to talk aloud to Jesus. But I also knew that as long as I yielded myself to Him and desired to pray, He would teach me to do so. He would give me the words to say.

Sheila and John McLeod were God's chosen ones to guide us and teach us in a very indirect way. They gave us many books and magazines to read. If ever I told Sheila my problems and heartaches and asked her to pray for me, she would sit down and talk to Jesus immediately. I know if anyone asked me to pray, I would do so at our family prayer time at night. I would say three Hail Mary's for them. But this talking to Jesus, any time and any place, in such a personal way, was something I had to learn.

And then .... all too soon, these good people decided it was time to leave India and return to Scotland. What were we going to do without them? Who would help us now? We soon had to realize that friends and family will leave us, but God will never ever leave us nor forsake us. He has promised us this in His Word and He will always keep His promises.

The McLeods presented us with a book, 'Prayers for the Common Man,' by William Barclay. With the help of this book, our family prayers became more meaningful. Instead of yawning through the Rosary and rattling off one mechanical prayer after another, without any meaning, we changed our mode of praying. We would read a portion of the Bible and then a very helpful and down-to-earth prayer from William Barclay's book. I encouraged the children to talk to Jesus in their own words. At first, it was difficult, but as we continued daily, we looked forward to these times together as a family. They certainly helped bring us closer to God and to one another.

But there were certain traditions we still clung to. We always added prayers for Daddy. "Please Jesus, take Daddy closer to You." And we would say three Hail Mary's for his soul and add, "Eternal rest grant unto him O Lord, and let perpetual light shine upon him. May his soul rest in peace with You Amen." I still believed with each Mass we offered for Percy, it was shortening his days in Purgatory and he was going closer to God. (That is something, I will come to later.)

With the help of William Barclay's book, we had now learned to pray spontaneously, even before the Charismatic movement had come to Poona. When we heard about these meetings, we were very keen to participate in them. A place was being sought to hold these meetings and I offered my home. After all, there was the Nursery furniture to cater to our needs. So we started the Charismatic meetings at '79.' Was **this** the reason Jesus wanted me to have the Nursery; so that I could use my place for His glory? Perhaps!

I remember the first meeting so clearly. As Bible passages were being announced, there was such a flutter of pages. We did not know where to find what! It was all so new to us. The meetings were really good. We learned new choruses and we were introduced to the Bible. We had a meaningful message from the Bible at every meeting and all of us felt very good. After the meetings, however, we were like deflated balloons. Why should this be? Why did we feel and act different at the meeting and then after it? Surely there was a solution to this. But what could it be? Perhaps time would tell!

Towards the end of 1975, I came across "The Hiding Place" by Corrie Ten Boom. It was really a fantastic book. It was Corrie's sister Betsie who amazed me. Facing persecutions and trials, but never a harsh word from her. Never did she have a bitter thought against anyone. Imagine lying in lice, being whipped...stripped naked, hardly any food to eat, and yet... yet, she could forgive these men who persecuted her and pray for them. What an amazing person!

By the time I came to the end of this book, I found myself on my knees crying to the Lord. My whole life flashed before me like a picture. There were certain pictures that stood out more than others. I cried with such deep repentance to the Lord asking for His forgiveness. I felt such a cleansing power go right through me. It was as if He, the *only* one who can cleanse us and forgive us our sins was standing there in front of me. I could feel His nail-pierced hand reach down and wipe away all those sins of mine forever. I rose from my knees feeling great. I was washed... I was cleansed.... I was whole!

CHAPTER 19

Christmas was in the air and around the corner! My children were seated round the dining table singing carols and cleaning the fruit for our Christmas cake.

"Come on children let us go for Confession," I called out to them. I got the shock of my life when they replied, "No Mama, we are not coming. We can confess our sins to Jesus." I admit I was rather taken aback with their response. I said, "Yes, yes I know, you can confess your sins to Jesus, but we have to go to Church and confess them to the priest. We have been brought up to do this and we will carry on doing so."

The children came to church with me. I won, or so I thought! But the Holy Spirit was at work in my heart unknowingly to me. As I drove, I wondered at my own behavior. How could I hang on to traditions so strongly, when only a few days before, I felt so thoroughly cleansed after confessing my sins to Jesus? It was a real tug of war of truth versus tradition. The Holy Spirit was surely working!

When we entered church, I brazenly went to a priest whom I had never ever gone to before, because I knew him too well. I knelt in the confessional and I opened my mouth. I knew for sure then, it was not me who spoke. What was I saying? "Bless me father, for I have sinned. I have confessed my sins to Jesus, and I believe He has forgiven me." I was shocked! I had not even planned to say this.

He looked at me and asked me, "Why did you come here?"

I replied, "To tell you this and to ask you for your blessing." Without a further word, he blessed me and told me to go in peace. As I returned to my place, I wondered why he did not say anything further to me. Perhaps he knows that this **is** the truth that it is Jesus alone to whom we should go and ask forgiveness for our sins. That was the last time I ever walked into a confessional!

'Out of the mouths of babes and infants…' These children of mine were no longer babes or infants, but they had been exposed to the Bible in school. Somehow, certain truths were beginning to take shape in their minds. And they... were teaching me!

January 1976 brought the first team of "Friends and Followers" from Canada to Poona. A friend encouraged us to go for the meetings, which were held on St. Mary's Church grounds. We had to sing for a wedding that evening, but there was time to go for the meeting later. I persuaded the children to come with me that Sunday evening, not knowing myself what it would be like. Yet I felt it was going to be something very special to us as a family.

I had already experienced gradual changes taking place in my life. Still there was a great desire for more change. I felt that God was going to do something for our family that day. Robin, who was just fourteen years old at that time, said, "Mum, you go for the meeting today and if it is good, we will come tomorrow."

"Today is the day of salvation son, let us go as a family today. Who knows if there will be a tomorrow? If you do not like it Robin, do not come tomorrow, but please, please let us go today."

Not a word did I get from him in reply. When it was time to leave home, there was no sign of Robin anywhere. He had disappeared. I drove round the colony searching for him. At last I found him hiding behind one of the newly constructed houses. I coaxed him again to come and he agreed. I seemed to be sure of one thing. This was a special invitation from the Lord not only to me, but for the family also... *"If anyone is thirsty, let him come to me and drink."* (John 7: 37b).

We reached St. Mary's Church grounds and found a stage erected. Hundreds of chairs were neatly placed in rows. We managed to get a good place in the front. Twelve young people from Canada formed the team. They were touring India to share the Gospel message through songs, music, skits etc. What amazed us that it was absolutely F-R-E-E. It made me think it was like the gift of Salvation, which is free. But it was no point merely knowing about it like we did, it had to be received and accepted by each individual.

Besides being a good evening, watching their talents being used for God's glory, something was happening deep down in our hearts. I knew I would not be the same person after leaving the meeting that night. One of the songs that had a lasting impression on me was, "Jesus is coming to earth again what if He comes today?"

The girl who sang this song said with impressive confidence, "I know if Jesus comes today, I will go straight to Heaven and be with Him for all eternity."

How could she be so sure? Did these people not sin? Didn't they know they had to make their last confession? These and other thoughts went through my mind. As much as I felt attracted to all this, I knew it would take me a long, long time to prepare myself to be pure enough and perfect enough to go to Jesus and ask Him to enter my heart.

How wrong I was! I had not realized that I could not do the changing myself. All I needed was to go to Him just as I was.

"Just as I am without one plea
But that Thy Blood was shed for me
And that Thou bidst me come to Thee
O Lamb of God I come, I come."

As the team sang this hymn, numerous thoughts went through my mind. You mean I could go to Him just as I was? Right now? What about my sins? Didn't I have to become a better person first? Amazing! All I had to do was to acknowledge I was a sinner. I had to repent of all my sins and ask Jesus to forgive me. I then had to ask Him to enter my heart as my Lord and Savior.

It was too good to be true. So very simple. Too simple in fact! That is why we fight against this free gift of salvation. How ignorant I was all this time. I was trying to do things on my own. I tried to be good. I said my prayers, made Novenas, recited the Rosary daily. I went to Confession, Mass, and Communion. I performed all the rituals and I was considered to be a good Catholic. Yet the team members repeatedly said, "No religion can save you. No amount of good works can save you. Your good works are like filthy rags."

How dare they condemn our religion and the good we do? But I learned that whatever they said was not their own words. They spoke directly from God's Word.

"If your religion, traditions, good works, goodness and intellect were sufficient to give you eternal life," I heard them say, "then why was it necessary for Jesus to leave His home in Heaven? Why did He come to earth to suffer as He did? Why did He have to die a criminal's death on the cross? Yes, Jesus the sinless one came to take our sin so that through Him, we might become the righteous ones of God. He loved us so much that while we were yet sinners, He came down and died for us; so that we might be free, free from all our sin and guilt."

Salvation is a free gift, and has to be accepted by each one of us individually if it is to become our personal gift. During the meeting, we heard in no uncertain terms that our religion was not enough to save us. We needed to have a personal relationship with the Lord Jesus.

At the end of the meeting, we were asked if we wanted to invite Jesus into our hearts. If so, we should raise our hands. Something was burning within me, but I dared not raise my hand. Again the question was asked. There was no response. Soon my children and I started nudging each other and making signs. We all felt the desire to raise our hands, but something was holding us back.

The team then prayed aloud, sensing there were many in the crowd who wanted to make a commitment. I wondered if these people could look right into our hearts. They seemed to know exactly how we felt. As they kept praying and encouraging the crowd, very sheepishly our hands went up while our heads went lower. We were so conscious of the crowd behind us. If that was an effort, what was to come next, was worse.

All those who raised their hands were asked to walk up to the front so that the team members could pray for them. No thanks! I was all set to dash out and go straight home. We enjoyed the evening. We were touched and were ready to return the next day... but walk to the front. No, definitely not!

I mentioned earlier that I felt God was inviting us as a family that particular day. As we were trying to rush home, and get lost in the crowd, one of the team members came right up to us. She was the girl who had sung that song which got me thinking. She came and said, "Hi, I am Judy Klaasen. What is your name?" I told her and then introduced my children to her. She asked, "Do you love Jesus?"

"Sure," I replied.

"I mean when did you start loving Jesus?"

"All my life. I am a Catholic."

"No, when did you come to know Him?"

Could she not understand? I had told her I was a Catholic. And yet she kept on asking when, why, how. Imagine asking a baptized Roman Catholic all these questions! Then she said, "Would you like to know more about Jesus?" I wondered what else could she tell us. We seemed to know it all! We had learned it all in Catechism class in school. To oblige her (or so I thought,) we agreed to sit for a few minutes and listen to her.

Those few minutes stretched to hours and yet it was not enough! We could have sat there all night long and it would not have been sufficient. We searched the Scriptures together and she showed us one gem of truth after another. I soon realized that in spite of all my traditions and religious knowledge, although I knew **about** Jesus, I did not really **know** Him in a personal and intimate way.

Judy spelt out the fact that all of us are sinners and fall short of the glory of God... *"The wages of sin is death, but the gift of God is eternal life in Christ Jesus our Lord."* (Romans 6: 23). We had to confess our sins to Jesus and He would forgive us and cleanse us from all our unrighteousness. Judy reminded us that there was absolutely nothing that we could do to save ourselves. All our good deeds were like filthy rags.

Jesus was knocking at the door of our hearts, asking to come in. *"Behold! I stand at the door and knock. If anyone hears My voice and opens the door,*

I will come in and sup with him and he with Me." (Revelation 3: 20). "Jesus is knocking He will not push or force Himself," she added. If we asked Him He would come in and stay with us forever. Once He enters, He will never leave us.

We listened like little children. She then asked us if we wanted to invite Jesus into our hearts. Who do you think asked first? None other than Robin my son, who did not want to come for the meeting! Each one of us repented of our sins, asked Jesus to forgive us and then made a personal commitment by inviting Jesus into our hearts. No sooner did we do this, we felt the nearness of God as our Father. God was no longer a figure a great distance away. He was not Someone we were afraid of. He was so near, so very very near, to each one of us.

We learned that nobody could do this for anyone else. It is between the individual and Jesus. It is absolutely personal. What a memorable day that was -- January 4th 1976.

"Oh what a wonderful, wonderful day,
Day I will never forget!
After in darkness I wandered away,
Jesus my Savior I met.
Oh what a tender, compassionate friend
He met the need of my heart.
Shadows dispelling, with joy I am telling
He made all the darkness depart."]

CHAPTER 20

The greatest joy was that all four of us experienced this great gift on the same day. We now became a doubly bonded family. I understood now what Jesus meant when He told Nicodemus the religious ruler, *"No one can see the kingdom of God unless he is born again."* (John 3:3). Even being a religious ruler was no guarantee of entry into Heaven. The scales had dropped from my eyes. God had invited us as a family that day. He had fulfilled His plan, "You have not chosen Me. I have chosen you."

Why Master why? May we be worthy of Your calling, whatever You want of us as a family.... *"Choose for yourselves this day whom you will serve. But as for me and my household, we will serve the Lord."* This is taken from Joshua 24: 15. Now Scripture had new meaning for us. There was no need to ask who wanted to go for the meeting the following day. We were in our seats as early as possible every evening thereafter.

We sent a message round the neighborhood, encouraging everyone to attend these meetings. We wanted them to share the immense joy and peace we were experiencing.

After the meeting we would wait for Judy and lay all our problems before her. She would set us at ease by answering all our questions straight from God's Word. It was fantastic! Any and every question of ours would be answered from the Bible. I just wanted to read more and learn more of God's Word for myself. Would I ever know God's Word the way Judy knew it? I surely desired this with all my heart. I asked Judy if she and her friends ever sinned. When she told me as human beings they did, I asked her how then did she sing that song with such confidence and state that she was going straight to Heaven.

She opened our eyes to a wonderful truth. She said that no matter **what** religion we followed before, once we repented of our sins and accepted Jesus into our hearts as Lord and Savior, we too could have the guarantee of eternal life here on earth and in Heaven for all eternity.

How wonderful that sounded. We did not have to worry about our last confession, or whether we might go to Heaven or not. Here was an absolute guarantee available NOW. As humans, we would surely fall, but as God's Word tells us, when we confess our sins, He is faithful and just to forgive us our sins and cleanse us from all our wrongdoing.

It made so much sense. Yet, I am afraid to say, in the days that followed, the traditions of the past still kept tugging at me. Although I accepted the new Gospel truths there were times when I would start doubting.

Surprisingly, the question of confessing our sins to a priest became a major doubt again for some reason. I mentioned this to Judy and was I relieved when she explained this to me so clearly from the Bible. She said that in the Old Testament times, the High Priest was a mediator between man and God. Once a year, only he could go behind the veil to offer sacrifice on behalf of the sins of the people. But Jesus the High Priest came and completed the work once and for all when He sacrificed His life on the cross for the sins of the world. Before He died, He bowed His head and said, "It is finished," and immediately the temple veil was rent in two from top to bottom. Now we do not have to go to God through any priest, mediator or anyone else, but only through Jesus Christ.

We can go directly through Jesus, the One and only mediator to the Father. Jesus Himself said, " *I am the way and the truth and the life. No one comes to the Father except through Me.*" (John 14:6) It is Jesus who gave His life for us. Jesus who shed His Blood for us; Jesus who died and rose again and is now seated at the right hand of the Father interceding for us. It is this same Jesus who is our Mediator. No saints, no priest, nobody...not even His beloved mother can mediate for us.

"For there is One God and One Mediator between God and man, the man Christ Jesus, who gave Himself as a ransom for all men..." (1 Timothy 2:5)

I soon found that no matter how learned and eloquent a person is, the best way to judge his wisdom is to see if what he says is based on God's Word.

"Heaven and earth will pass away, but My words will never pass away." (Mark 13: 31.) Judy taught us real nuggets of truth from God's Word. We were so hungry. We devoured as much as we could daily.

All too soon, that week came to an end. What would we do? The Friends and Followers were leaving us. How would we grow spiritually? Who would answer all our questions?? I will never forget what Judy said to us. "We are going, that is true, but I want you to know that Jesus will remain with you always. The same Jesus, who will go along with us, will be here with you. He has promised never to leave you nor forsake you. Remember, He is true to His Word."

She told us we were like new born babes. Just as babies need milk regularly to grow, we also need to have our food – God's Word - the Bible, regularly to grow spiritually. It was a sad farewell, but praise God, we had His Word with us. No matter what happened, or how tired we felt, we read His Word daily, both day and night.

I soon found many more changes taking place in my life. There was no visible teacher to guide or lead me, but certainly, as I read God's Word, I was being convicted of a number of failings in my life. By whom? Who was my teacher? Jesus had said, *"The Counselor, the Holy Spirit whom the Father will send in My name, will teach you all things."* (John 14: 26) So I had the very best teacher in the Holy Spirit Himself.

The more I read the Bible, the more I found we were doing things we should not be doing and were not doing things we should be doing. There was absolute confusion in my mind and heart. I tried asking a few priests some questions that were troubling me, but I could not receive a satisfactory answer. For months, there was a great struggle within me and God was watching. God was waiting for His perfect time.

CHAPTER 21

"Therefore, if anyone is in Christ, he is a new creation; the old has gone, the new has come!" (2 Corinthians 5:17)

After inviting Jesus into my heart and being 'born again' I realized I was a new creation. My old life had to pass away. Whereas formerly I would pray to saints and make Novenas to Mary, I knew I could not do this any longer. I had been convicted through God's Word that Jesus is the **only** mediator. I was also convinced that His glory could not be shared with anyone else...nobody! The Bible teaches that all of us are sinners and all of us fall short of the glory of God. That meant Mary too had fallen short of His glory and needed His saving grace.

Mary was a good and pious maiden, someone to be respected and admired. God chose her to be the mother of Jesus the Man. Jesus had two distinct natures: divine and human. Mary was chosen to be His mother when He took the form of Man. But then

I recalled we used to pray to her as Mother of God. The Holy Spirit sent from God, showed me this was not right. I knew now that I could definitely never ever recite the Hail Mary again and address her as the Mother of God. I had not even given this a second thought before. I knew I could never bow in front of her picture or statue as was customary after the Novena services.

One of the commandments God gave Moses clearly states: *"I am the Lord your God, who brought you out of Egypt, out of the land of slavery. You shall have no other gods before Me. You shall not make for yourself an idol in the form of anything in Heaven above or in the earth beneath or in the waters below. You shall not bow down to them and worship them; for I, the LORD your God, am a jealous God, punishing the children for the sin of the fathers to the third and fourth generation of those who hate Me, but showing love to a thousand generations of those who love Me and keep My commandments."* (Exodus 20:2-6).

That was enough for me. I needed nothing further to convict and convince me that I **had** to stop praying to Mary. Even my hourly Novenas to the Infant Jesus of Prague came to an end, because the Bible warns us about the vain repetition of prayers. (Matthew 6:7)

After inviting Jesus into our hearts, we used to hold Bible studies at home on Sundays with some friends after Mass. We were keen to study and search the Scriptures. Here again, it was getting rather confusing. God was surely dealing with us and teaching us new lessons each time we met.

Soon our weekly prayer meetings at home became more meaningful. I found the good feeling that had lasted only during the meeting, could now last every moment of every day. I found I was a new person now, because of what Jesus had done and was doing in my heart and life.

I did not have to be one kind of person at the meeting and another type out of it. **Jesus in me**... made all the difference.

The Catholic Charismatic Group continued their meetings in our home. More and more people attended these meetings. We were informed that we would have a seminar on "The Life in the Spirit." This comprised of a number of meetings to prepare us for the Baptism of the Holy Spirit. I can still recall my response to this. "I have Jesus...I do not need the Spirit." I felt so content with what I had. I did not feel the urgency to want any more or to grow any more. I thought that was **IT**. But some very good books fell into my hands. God's perfect timing, no doubt. In one of them, I had read how the disciples did not want Jesus to leave them. He told them it was necessary for Him to go, so that He could send His Spirit to them.

The more I read, the more I realized that even though the disciples lived and had such a close walk with Jesus, yet they too were so weak. All of them had deserted Him in the end. Peter had thrice denied ever knowing Jesus. Yet Jesus loved and forgave him. Even though the disciples deserted Jesus, He forgave them and met with them when He rose from the dead.

Before Jesus ascended into heaven, He told them to wait and pray for the gift the Father would send them. As they waited and prayed in the Upper Room, together with Mary and other believers, they received the gift of the Holy Spirit. Then those weak, timid men became bold and powerful witnesses for Christ. They brought thousands of people into the Kingdom. Acts 1:8 tells us clearly: *"When the Holy Spirit comes upon you, you will be filled with power and you will be My witnesses."*

If this was gospel truth, who was I to say I did not want the infilling of the Holy Spirit? I learned that when I asked Jesus into my heart, His Spirit came to dwell within me. But now I prayed and repented and asked the Lord to prepare my heart for the Baptism of the Holy Spirit, where the Holy Spirit would come upon me and empower me.

After we completed the seminar, our prayer group spent a day at the Lord's feet in the Convent of Jesus and Mary. We studied from God's Word from Luke 11:13, *"If you then, though you are evil, know how to give good gifts to your children, how much more will your Father in Heaven give the Holy Spirit to those who ask Him!"* And so, we asked God to fill us with His Holy Spirit. Since Jesus said, *" When you ask you will receive,"* we truly believed we had received.

What tremendous joy filled my soul. I felt a deep cleansing and infilling and over flowing of God's Spirit within me. I felt clean...pure...holy. I returned home that evening walking on a cloud. I was in close communion with the Triune God, as I had sweet fellowship with my Maker before retiring that night.

I was suddenly woken in the early hours of the morning. I felt someone shake my shoulder gently yet firmly. I heard a voice saying, "Go tell everyone. Give the Good News to the world." I wondered what kind of a dream this was. I turned over and tried to sleep again, but the same command came twice over. I knew then that this was not a dream, but God speaking to me. **Me**? Go tell everyone? How Lord? Who was I? All these questions followed in quick succession. But I knew if this were a command from God, He would give me the correct words and the grace to spread His message. It was just four o'clock in the morning. I picked up my pen and paper and went to the next room, as I did not want to disturb the children.

After much prayer, I put pen to paper. I just knew this was definitely from the Lord, because my hand moved so fluently. I wrote with His help and guidance, about our meetings and how we had prepared for our Baptism. I added how essential it was to obey Jesus and receive the Baptism of the Holy Spirit. I was so wide-awake as I continued writing what I was led to write.

A copy of this article was published in " The New Covenant" a Catholic Charismatic magazine in Bombay. It was also published in "The Venture" the Poona Diocesan paper. Once it was published, I sent copies to all my friends and relations scattered in different parts of the world. So in this way, I had obeyed the Lord and spread the news all over the world. I did not realize that this was only the beginning!

CHAPTER 22

The closer my walk with the Lord was, I found I had more problems to face. But has not Jesus promised us peace that passeth all understanding? Yes! He has promised us peace, but we must get this clear…He gives us peace even through the difficult situations we have to face.

I had to face some difficult problems with school parents. Every year a number of them would withdraw their children from the school without paying their fees. Some would be extremely rude and even threaten me, but I knew I was not alone. I could depend on God to protect me always. He has said in His Word, *"I have summoned you by name, you are Mine. When you pass through deep waters, I will be with you; and when you pass through the rivers, they will not sweep over you. When you walk through the fire, you will not be burned; the flames will not set you ablaze. For I am the Lord your God, the Holy One of Israel, your Savior."* (Isaiah 43:2-3).

There will certainly be problems in our lives, but we do not have to face them alone. He is with us every step of the way; just as He was with Daniel in the lions' den and with Daniel's three friends in the fiery furnace.

Shortly after I had surrendered my life to the Lord, I found the numbers in my Nursery had fallen rapidly; from over thirty pupils I now had nineteen. My income decreased. How would I manage to make ends meet? My children would ask Jesus to send me more pupils. I would pray like this: "Dear Jesus, if You think I need this short respite from coping with extra pupils, I accept it as Your will. But you know Lord; I have so many bills to pay and my children to look after. Lord, how can I cope? Since You are my Lord, my bills are Your bills; so please Lord, find some other way of paying them for me. Thank You Lord."

And that is exactly what He did. We experienced miracle after miracle. We had no idea where the gifts came from, that is, from which human source. But we certainly knew the Main Source! God's Mighty Hand was behind it all. We had not mentioned our plight to anyone. Yet through the post, a cheque would come with a note enclosed: "A small gift from the Lord." Sometimes an envelope would be pushed into the front room with some cash and an assurance of God's faithfulness. Rations and fresh food would be put into my car in school, just when I was at rock bottom. (This I learned later, was from my very good friend Roshani Bharucha.) God was proving His greatness to us over and over again. And we were amazed.

It taught us to increase our faith and trust in Him completely, at all times and in all situations. Our mighty God is so faithful. He is our Jehovah Jireh, our provider. He always supplied all our needs.

At times, I would not know what I would serve for the next meal but Jesus would always intervene. Sometimes my children would need money for some expense in school. It would have to be submitted by a certain date. They would ask me for it and with a broad, confident smile, I would assure them they would get the cash on time. They would then ask, "Mum, do you have the money?" Being caught off guard, I would tell them that I did not have it right then, but I would definitely give it to them on time. When they questioned further I would tell them to have faith and Jesus would give it to us. And give it He did. Always.

"Great is Thy faithfulness,

Great is Thy faithfulness,

Morning by morning new mercies I see.

All I have needed Thy hand has provided,

Great is Thy faithfulness, Lord unto me."

Life had so much meaning now. I was really experiencing the abundant life...life in all its fullness, which Jesus has promised us in His Word in John 10:10.

I had wondered why God had saved me from those three accidents in 1969. It took me seven years to find the answer. He saved me physically so that He could save me spiritually. He saved my life so that I could have the assurance of eternal life by trusting and believing Jesus as my Lord and Savior.

It was wonderful living each day with Him and for Him. Whatever problems and difficulties we had to face, there was no need to get into a frenzy. He was always there to help us and see us through.

CHAPTER 23

If people in Poona forgot my face, they remembered me because of my lovely, black ramshackle car. She looked quite a disgrace now, our little Morris Minor. She sure needed a coat of paint. We loved her all the same. More often than not, she was at the mechanic's, needing some repairs or the other; but to us she was our beloved 'Black Beauty.' I still remember telling Percy I would never get rid of her. I would always keep her for sentimental reasons. If only she could speak, that car would speak volumes!

I remember how she first came into our lives. One day Percy came to my quarters at the N.D.A. His grin was wider than his face could hold.

"I am buying a car Marge. Now we can go out whenever we want. She's a beaut Marge. She is black and shiny. She has a luggage carrier. Guess what? There is even a canvas bucket in the front." He bubbled with excitement and went on describing this car.

"What is the bucket for Perce?"

"You know Marge, when we go on long drives and the radiator gets over heated, we will have water at hand for it."

"That is all very well, Perce, but where is the money coming from to buy it?"

"Oh that is all thought of Marge. I am going to borrow the amount from Dad." And so he did, and 'Black Beauty' became an intimate part of our lives.

Every weekend, we would bundle into her with our picnic lunch ready to drive to the ends of the earth together. Having a radio in the car was an added bonus. If we were not chatting and laughing, we were singing along with the Binaca Hit Parade. "Cindy oh Cindy," "Jamaican Farewell," "Green Door," "Scarlet Ribbon," were the top of the hits those days. We enjoyed hearing these songs over the radio as we drove to the foot of Sinaghad Fort or to the periphery of the N.D.A. to Vithalwadi or our Blueberry Hill (Ramtekdi). We covered miles in our 'Black Beauty'. If our car was precious to us during our courting days, she was even more so on our honeymoon. 'Black Beauty' was a part of the family and went with us almost everywhere.

After we settled in Poona, Percy tried to teach me to drive. Neutral...switch on...start...accelerate...I had to remember these instructions and more each time. Pressing the accelerator and releasing the clutch was a trial. What a patient instructor Percy was. I would lose my patience each time. When I noticed an extra cyclist or bullock cart on the road, I would shout in alarm. I expected the whole road to be empty for me! In spite of that, I still enjoyed my driving lessons.

But to drive solo...I simply refused. Why did I need to, when Percy was always there?

Now, I would never have Percy by my side. Oh, how would I manage? Would I dare to drive alone now? No, not me! So I went against my word and put 'Black Beauty' up for sale. She was flown to Poona from Chandigarh with the rest of our luggage. Even though I said I would always keep her, circumstances had changed. I could not drive and I needed the money. Fortunately, I was not offered a good price for her.

While in Bombay, my father in law brought up the subject of the car. If ever he gave me good advice, it was that day. "**Do not** ever sell that car," he told me. "You are about to build your house. You will need to rush up and down to the site often. Think of the difficulty in getting transport whenever you need it. Keep the car. It will be a saving in the long run." Words of knowledge and wisdom from my father in law. I suppose I just wanted a little persuasion to keep it.

I kept her parked in a friend's garage in Poona. I dared not venture out on my own. When my Dad stayed with me and helped me to set up home in the Southern Command Mess, he was only too happy to drive me about. He enjoyed driving me and I enjoyed being driven! Then Cedric my brother in law came and made me drive again. He restored my confidence. When you have to do something and there is nobody to help you... you knuckle down and do it. With daily practice on the Race Course, I mastered reversing and everything else.

It was little wonder that I grew to love 'Black Beauty' even more. When I could not manage her up a slope, I would bend forward and tap her on the side and say, "Come on babe, I know you can do it." The children would be amused by my efforts in persuading 'Black Beauty.'

It was difficult to manage her upkeep, but at least we could go out together as a family. It certainly would have cost much more if we had to depend on other transport. But something unforeseen happened. There was an announcement in the newspapers that all those with foreign vehicles had to pay an additional tax. I did not think my 'Black Beauty' came under this category. She was so old and weather-beaten by now. So I did not pay heed to this notice. With the result, when I went to pay my tax, I received a rude shock. The R.T.O. informed me that I had to pay double tax plus a fine for the previous year. The amount seemed colossal. I was nearly in tears. I asked the Officer to come and see my car and decide whether I came under this category or not. He was most sympathetic but told me I had to abide by the rules and pay the tax and pay it soon, or else the fine would increase.

I came home and whom could I turn to but to my dearest friend Jesus Himself. I cried my heart out to Him, asking Him what I should do. I opened His Word for comfort and my eyes fell on Psalm 34. *" I sought the Lord and He answered me; He delivered me from all my fears."* I felt so good just talking it over with Him. I wanted Him to speak to me through His Word.

As I turned the pages, I came across a familiar verse: *"Do not store up for yourselves treasures on earth, where moth and rust destroy, and where thieves break in and steal. But store up for yourselves treasure in Heaven, where moth and rust do not destroy... for where your treasure is there your heart will be also."* (Matthew 6: 19-21.)

"Lord," I cried, "what are You trying to say to me? Do You want me to sell the car? Tell me Lord." I was willing to obey Him and do whatever He commanded. As I prayed, I did not think this is what He meant. At that time, I used the car so much for the Lord's work. I used to take some friends to pay weekly visits to the Widows' Home and Mother Teresa's Home, to share Christ's love with the inmates. Then what **did** the Lord mean by these earthly treasures?

Suddenly my hand went to my neck. I realized what He meant. My eyes then traveled to my hands. I wasted no time. I got into the car and went straight to the jewelers. I sold my gold chain and bangles, which my mother in law had given me on my wedding day. I now had enough to pay for the tax and my fine, as well as have some cash left over.

Each time my bills mounted, I knew it was no good storing up any treasures on this earth. I made one trip after the other to the jewelers till eventually there was nothing more to sell, not even my wedding ring!

CHAPTER 24

In October 1976, there was news of a big Charismatic convention at Bombay. Everyone was preparing for it and planning to attend.

I too longed to go for the Convention, but there was a snag. We could not leave the house at that time, as we had no servant. Besides that, we had two dogs to be cared for. I really felt disappointed that I could not attend this convention. However, nothing happens in our lives without our Father being aware of it.

A few days later, I read in the local newspaper "The Poona Herald" that there was a convention being held at the New Life Center in Poona. The remarkable thing was that it was to be held at the very same time as the Bombay Convention. I said, "It is the same Word of God being preached, so let us go here." And go we did! The four of us and two other friends.

I had never heard God's Word preached in such a powerful and dynamic way before. I was literally hanging onto every single word. The following evening we attended again, to hear nuggets of truth explained to us. We knew the Lord had kept us back for a purpose known to Him.

We heard there were morning meetings, but we had no intention of attending them. One morning, however, I felt the urgency to go for the meeting. I was so taken aback at the solid teaching from the Book of Revelation. I realized we knew so little. There was so much to learn. After that morning, we decided to attend the morning meetings as well.

The next morning, there was a discourse on "God's Word and Obedience." I can still remember the gist of what the preacher said. He told us that God speaks to us through His Word: 'Logos.' Then He confirms it through various means. It may be through a person, a book, or a message. Once we hear **God's Word** and it has been confirmed that God is speaking to us, we must put it into **Human Action**. Even though the command may seem strange to us at times, we must obey it nevertheless. In so doing, we will have to face a **Crisis**, whatever it may be.

He gave us an example of "The Wedding Feast at Cana" when the wine ran out. Mary the mother of Jesus told the servants, "Whatever He tells you to do, do it."

The preacher said, that Jesus told the servants, "Fill the pots with water and take them out." **God's Word.** They had to fill the pots with water and take them out . . . **Human Action.** A strange command indeed, as the master of ceremonies needed wine and not water. Here these servants were told to carry the water pots out and give it to him. They would have to face the consequences of their action at the hands of the master...**the Crisis**. No matter how strange God's command may seem to us, we must put it into human action, no matter what crisis we will have to face.

The servants obeyed and everyone knows that such good wine was never ever tasted before. That is obedience. Do not question God. When He commands you to do something, just trust and obey, for there is no other way.

With this lecture on 'obedience' deeply imprinted on my mind and heart, I knew exactly what to say to a young medical student who had been attending the evening meetings. Nearly every day, during the course of the sessions, points on Salvation, Water Baptism and Baptism of the Holy Spirit were discussed. When I reflected on this, I was quite happy to know I had the gift of Salvation when I had asked Jesus into my heart as Lord and Savior. I ticked the next point off in my mind. I was baptized as an infant with water...so that meant I had Water Baptism. I had already received the Baptism of the Holy Spirit. So all that was needed for me now, was to grow closer and closer to Jesus daily. Or so I thought!

This Catholic medical student Darryl, * came and told me that he was convicted that he should get baptized. "Whatever for?" was my immediate response. "We are already baptized. Why do you want to get baptized again?" I asked. He replied that God had convicted him through His Word and he must obey. Since he was so determined and convicted, I shared what we had learned in the morning session. He repeated that God had spoken to him very clearly through His Word. He told me that had read certain verses that had convicted him but we did not go into detail. If he was convicted, so be it. I certainly was not!

Now human action had to be taken. I asked him if he had informed his parents and the priest. He had done so. Then what about the crisis he would have to face? I told him he might have to face rejection from others and that he might be excommunicated from the Catholic Church. He seemed to be aware of all this and yet, was willing to go ahead and obey the Lord all the way. I wished him all the best and prayed with him. Yet, I was not at all convinced that I should be water baptized. I was absolutely satisfied with my Infant Baptism. In fact, a day was set-aside for Baptisms during the convention, but I refused to witness this event, as I did not see the necessity of it. I was content with what I believed.

On the final day of the convention, no mention was made of Baptism. It was a wonderful meeting and a powerful message was preached. I just wanted to surrender myself completely and go all out to follow and obey the Lord. I asked the children and our friends to come forward with me to the speaker so that he could pray for us. I wanted to be open to God's will in our lives and obey Him in all things.

As we thanked the preacher for his ministry to us, I heard myself suddenly asking him about Water Baptism. Even after he explained to us, I mentioned that we were baptized as infants. I was quite taken aback when he asked me to show him in the Bible where it was the practice for infants to be baptized. I could not do this, I must confess. He went on to say that in the Bible we read that people always repented first and then got baptized voluntarily. They were aware of what they were doing.

I asked, "Do you mean to say our baptism is not valid then?" He replied, "It is not what I say or anyone else says, what matters is what God's Word says to us." He mentioned that Jesus was taken to the temple with His parents not to be baptized but to be **presented** and **dedicated** to God. God gives parents the gift of a child and they should go with thanksgiving in their hearts and dedicate this child to God. Baptism comes later, when the individual knowingly and willingly repents of sin and publicly declares to follow Christ through the Waters of Baptism.

He told us that Baptism does not save a person. "You can go in a dry sinner and come out a wet one; so also Infant Baptism could never save or purify anyone. Baptism does not make a person a Christian. The most important factor is to repent, to turn away from the old self and publicly confess you want to follow Jesus all the way by being obedient to Him. Since this is His command, we must obey Him," he smiled and told us.

As I listened, thoughts raced through my mind. I voiced a few of them aloud. What would my Church say? What about the Charismatic Group held in my house? The preacher said, "Trust in God. Do not cross your bridges till you come to them." We agreed we needed to obey God wholeheartedly. If this was God's Will for us, we certainly wanted to obey Him and be baptized. We wanted to do all He would have us do. But we could get baptized at a later date.

Just then the preacher said, "So you can come tomorrow to be baptized."

"Tomorrow? W w w...what?" I stammered in response.

I nearly chickened out there and then. Surely that was too soon? After all, this was a big decision we were going to make. The preacher advised us to go home and pray about it. That is exactly what we did.

We were given a booklet on 'Water Baptism.' We went home that night and read through each and every Scripture reference. We prayed much and left ourselves completely open to God's Will in our lives.

I had certain premonitions I shared with the children. I told them by taking this step we might be shunned and ostracized. I felt the children would not be invited out and accepted by the youth group in the neighborhood. My joy knew no bounds when they said they did not mind that at all. All they wanted to do was to obey God, no matter what the cost.

I wondered whether we should tell the parish priest about our decision. On second thoughts, I said that we had not asked his permission when we asked Jesus to come into our hearts. Neither had we asked his permission to receive the Baptism of the Holy Spirit. Then why ask him now? This was something absolutely personal between Almighty God and each one of us. And so, I decided not to approach the priest just then.

CHAPTER 25

The next day dawned October 24th 1976. And with the sun, numerous doubts started rising in my soul. Should we really go ahead with our Water Baptism? "Lord, if this is Your will, please give me a sign." Every time I opened the Bible, I would open to some reference about Baptism. The first was a reference from Acts 2. On the day of Pentecost the people were troubled and asked Peter and the other apostles, "What shall we do?" and in verse 38, Peter replied, *"Repent and be baptized everyone of you, in the name of Jesus Christ for the forgiveness of your sins. And you will receive the gift of the Holy Spirit."* In verse 41 we read, *"Those who accepted this message were baptized and about three thousand were added to their number that day."*

I opened then to Acts 10 and read about Peter at Cornelius' house. While Peter was speaking, the gift of the Holy Spirit had been poured on these Gentile people. In verse 47, Peter said, *"Can anyone keep these people from being baptized with water? They have received the Holy* Spirit *just as we have."* And they too were baptized.

In Acts 8, I read about Philip and the Ethiopian official. Philip had been led by the Spirit to meet this man as he was returning from Jerusalem in his chariot, reading aloud from the Book of Isaiah. Philip ran up to him and explained the scripture he was reading. He told him the good news of Jesus. In verse 36 we read that, *"As they traveled along the road, they came to some water and the eunuch said, 'Look here is water. Why shouldn't I be baptized?'... Then Philip and the eunuch went down into the water and Philip baptized him."*

I had asked the Lord for a sign and He kept on giving me different verses on Baptism from the Bible. What patience our loving Savior has. The time passed and soon it was evening. It was time for us to pack our case with a change of clothes. And still I dared to say, "Lord, could You please show me for the **very** last time, if this is what You truly want us to do. I do want to obey You Lord, but is this YOU speaking to me?"

I wanted to be absolutely certain.

You could have knocked me down with a feather. I opened to Matthew 3:13 -17, which speaks about the Baptism of Jesus Himself. Oh! I had to ask the Lord to forgive me for my doubting mind and my lack of faith. If Jesus, the perfect, sinless Son of God went through the Waters of Baptism because He wanted to do all that was right, then who was I to question any further? I just knew that this was more than a confirmation. I **had** to trust and obey.

God had spoken to me through **His Word** so clearly. Now I had to put it into **Human Action** and then I would have to face the **Crisis**, whatever it would be.

Before we could leave home, the doorbell rang and in came an Anglican priest. He had never called on us before, so it surprised me when he came that day. In the course of conversation, I asked him what he thought of Water Baptism. He told me he fully believed in it. Immediately I asked him "Are you baptized?" He replied in the negative. I turned to him and said, "Strange, you believe in it, you know it is right then how is it you are not baptized?" This man of God surprised me when he said, "What will my church say? It is not accepted by them." It really shocked me that this priest was more concerned with man's opinion rather than going ahead with what God wanted. Anyway, praise God, after some time, I rejoice to say he took the bold step of following the Lord through the Waters of Baptism.

To go back to that memorable evening. This priest was returning to a hill station close by with a teacher who was known to us. I requested him not to share about our Baptism with her. Then on second thoughts, I said, "If the Lord leads you to talk about it then go ahead. Just follow His leading."

Now we had all the confirmation we needed. There was no turning back and definitely no more asking for further signs. It was time to leave. Four of us and our two friends went to New Life Center. We met our two medical student friends, Darryl and Ashok. We assembled round the tank with the rest of the congregation and sang songs of worship to the Lord.

One by one we got into the water and publicly confessed our beliefs. We proclaimed we wanted to follow and obey Jesus. It was such a wonderful experience confessing Him before the others present. Our joy knew no bounds as we were buried to our old selves, completely immersed in the water, and then we rose up and got out of the tank. We were thrilled to obey the Lord.

At first, we kept our Baptism a secret. We did not want to share it with anyone, except with a very few people who were close to us and who believed as we did. But they were scared to follow suit, even though they knew it was the correct thing to do. They had no idea how it would be accepted in their homes and what repercussions they would have to face, once their parents were aware of what they had done.

Then the Lord convicted me that we were not to keep quiet about our Baptism any longer. We had done nothing wrong. We had obeyed the Lord and now the time was ripe for us to tell others about it. We had to take a bold stand for the truth and we would have to face whatever persecution there was to face for His Name's sake.

CHAPTER 26

A few Sundays later, while I was sitting in Church, I said, "Lord, if You think it is time for me to tell the parish priest about our Baptism, please send him home this week." That was quite a fleece to put before the Lord, because this priest had not come home for almost three months. Three days after I prayed, he visited us. I just knew it was an answer to prayer and it was time for me to share my doubts with him. We commenced with a prayer and I brought out God's Word to be our guide, as we discussed various matters. There were many issues that were bothering and confusing me. The more I read the Bible the more confused I became. We were laying so much stress on things that we were not supposed to be doing according to the Bible and vice versa.

My first question was about the Mass. The Catholics believe that the Mass is most essential. It is supposed to be the Sacrifice of Calvary enacted daily. The only difference is that on the Cross - Jesus shed His blood, whereas the Mass is an unbloody sacrifice. The bread and wine they say become the very body and blood of Jesus at the consecration when the priest recites the sacred words, "This is my body," and "This is my blood."

In 1 Corinthians chapter 11 verses 23 to 26, we read what Jesus did at the Last Supper. Verse 26 says, *"For whenever you eat this bread and drink this cup, you proclaim the Lord's death until He comes."* If this was a command of Jesus, I wondered WHY we did not obey it specifically, especially if the Mass was so very important. Only the priest drinks the wine while the congregation is given a host (thin wafer). "Well Margaret," he explained, "it is because there are such large numbers in the church that there will not be enough to go around." I stared aghast at his kind, shiny face. I could not believe what I was hearing. "But then, what did Jesus say? Are we to obey man or Jesus?"

No reply!

In Hebrews 9: 25 to 28, we read, *"Nor did He enter heaven to offer Himself again and again, the way the high priest enters the Most Holy Place every year with blood that is not His own. Then Christ would have to suffer many times since the creation of the world. But now He has appeared once and for all at the end of the ages to do away with sin by the sacrifice of Himself. Just as man is destined to die once, and after that to face the judgment, so Christ was sacrificed once to take away the sins of many people..."*

In Hebrews 10: 10 to 14, *"We have been made holy through the sacrifice of the body of Jesus Christ once and for all. Day after day every priest stands and performs his religious duties; again and again he offers the same sacrifices, which can never take away sins. But when this priest had offered for all time one sacrifice for sins, He sat down at the right hand of God. Since that time He waits for His enemies to be made His footstool, because by one sacrifice He has made perfect forever those who are being made holy."*

I realized that Jesus had done it once and for all. There was no need to repeat the sacrifice over and over again. I realized it was not essential to attend the sacrifice of the Mass any longer.

We had been taught that if we missed Mass on a Sunday or on a day of obligation, it was a 'mortal' sin. But the Bible clearly states that Christ had **completed** the sacrifice once and for all. In fact, nowhere in the Bible does it state that Jesus or the Apostles ever said Mass or celebrated it. Instead, in the Book of Acts Chapter 2, we read about the believers who met together in the temple courts every day. They broke bread in their homes and ate together with glad, sincere hearts, "praising God and enjoying the favor of all the people."

The statues all over the Church also raised a question in my mind, especially after reading Exodus 20: 4-5. *"You shall not make for yourself an idol in the form of anything in Heaven above or on the earth beneath or in the waters below. You shall not bow down to them or worship them; for I, the Lord your God, am a jealous God."* I was also convicted when I read about idols from the book of Isaiah 44: 9-17. In verse 9 it reads, *"What fools they are who manufacture idols for their gods. Their hopes remain unanswered. They themselves are witnesses that this is so, for their idols neither see nor know. No wonder those who worship them are so ashamed."*

After asking Jesus to be my Lord and Savior, I got rid of all my medals, holy pictures and statues. His Word had convicted me and so I obeyed. When I questioned the priest about statues, he told me that they were there to aid people in their worship and devotion. Again, I had to draw his attention to what God's Word so clearly said about it. Why did we do things, which were contrary to God's Word, I wondered.

For thirteen years, ever since my husband died, I would offer a Mass for him every month. Even though I was not earning much money and the cost of Masses had increased, I still paid for these Masses, thinking they would shorten Percy's days in Purgatory. But Hebrews 9:27 says *"Just as a man is destined to die once, and after that to face judgment."*

If this is so, my question was, "Why do we need to give Masses for the dead?" What a blind fool I had been all these years. The sacrifice of Jesus is free, freely given to save us. We have the guarantee that our sins are washed away and we can have eternal life right here and now if we repent of our sins and believe and trust in Jesus. Here was I literally trying to pay for Percy's freedom after he was dead and already judged, by giving Masses for his soul.

On reading the Bible further, I read in Psalm 73, how the rich have all the good things in life and the poor have to suffer. I thought that when these rich people die they could still have it good, as their relations could afford to pay for any number of Masses for their souls. What about the poor people? They find it so hard to exist when alive what more when they are dead? Who can afford to give Masses for their souls? When I posed this question to another priest he assured me that the poor people were prayed for. I wanted to know why all people could not be treated alike in death. Why should anyone 'buy' Masses for the dead?

His reply shocked me. He said, "Don't you think we priests have to live?" This made me think of how Jesus had fed five thousand men besides women and children with five loaves and two fish. I told him this and I also said God tells us in His Word we are not to worry about our food and our clothes. If we seek His kingdom and His righteousness then all these *'things'* will be given to us. I told this priest he did not really have to depend on money from Masses for the dead to survive. God would provide, if he would truly trust and obey the Lord. Naturally he did not like what I said to him and showed his objection. If only he believed in tithes, and knew what God promises us in Malachi 3:10.

These were few of the questions I raised, but I did not receive any concrete answers or help. God's Word on the other hand is solid and unchangeable. It is something I can rely on, come what may.

Then came the bombshell. I told the priest about our Baptism and the reason why we got baptized. He could not understand why we needed to do that. He replied that a few months earlier some people had approached him and said they were praying that our family would not leave the Catholic Church. I was stunned, because it had never entered my mind to do so then. Even with all these doubts in my mind, I never dreamt of leaving the Catholic Church. I wondered if by the end of our time together, he would pass the verdict that I was excommunicated.

Instead, he said, "Margaret, I can see you are very close to God and you are obeying Him. Carry on...but -- please do not speak to others and tell them what you are doing."

To that I replied, "I am sorry father, just as I prayed to God about speaking to you, I will pray and be guided WHO to speak to, WHAT to speak, and WHEN to speak."

This conversation took place at the end of November 1976. We continued going to the Catholic Church every Sunday. Straight after this, however, we would rush to the other end of town to attend the service at the New Life Center. We were eager to learn more from God's Word. The Lord's Day was truly spent in His Presence now.

Previously, after Church, the time would be spent in preparing food for our bodies, but now, we were more concerned about food for our souls. We got real solid teaching at the New Life Center from Pastor Timothy John.

Formerly, if a sermon lasted for more than ten minutes, we would be looking at our watches and wondering when it would end. Here at N.L.C. the meetings used to go on till one or two o'clock in the afternoon and it did not tire us. It was such a blessing.

In January 1977, there was a Convention at Hume Church in Bombay. This time, we had someone to care for our home and dogs, so we were able to attend this convention. We stayed at the Nagpada Neighborhood House, in the adjoining compound. The evening before the convention commenced, we visited a friend of ours at Mazagaon.We had a long wait at the bus stop on our return. There was quite a crowd waiting for the bus. As we were getting into the bus, I felt someone push me and tug at my bag. Looking down, I found my bag was closed, so thought nothing more about it. The bus fare was in my pocket. After paying for our tickets, I continued to cling to my bag.

When we reached Hume Church, I went to the bookstall to buy a Bible for my brother Noel. My purse was not in my bag! My face grew paler as I searched every compartment of the bag. Whoever committed the crime, managed to push me, open my bag, take the wallet out and then close it in record time. I sheepishly put the Bible down. I was left penniless. Fortunately, we had already paid for our stay, as soon as we had arrived. Instead of being upset, I was inspired to compose a verse praising God, in spite of what had happened. By doing this and really meaning it, I felt uplifted. We mentioned the theft to just a few friends. Soon word went round and many brothers and sisters in the Lord came to our rescue. They were so generous. Some gave us money; others brought us food and fruit. In fact, we had much more than we could have bought with the money we had. Our Heavenly Father truly provides much much more than our needs, if only we trust Him and seek Him with all our hearts.

We were more than blessed at that Convention and returned to Poona feeling so much closer to Jesus. I must mention a wonderful thing that happened during the convention. The morning after I had been pick-pocketed, I phoned Noel and told him about it. I ended my conversation by saying, "Praise God, He is great."

He said, "How can you ever praise God for this? I just do not understand you!" I replied, "It does not matter what happens, but I will always praise God." He must have thought I was bonkers. I persuaded him to come for the evening meeting. He said, "I cannot promise and anyhow, I do not think I can make it." We prayed very much, however, that he would come.

We were extremely happy in the evening, when we saw that Noel had arrived for the meeting. At the end of the session, there was an altar call for those who wanted to commit their lives to the Lord. I could have screamed with delight, when I saw Noel walking up to make his commitment to the Lord and to ask Jesus to come into his heart. Oh, how we rejoiced that he was convicted to do this by the leading of God's Holy Spirit.

The next afternoon, during the lunch break, we rushed to Juhu to visit my parents and share the Good News with them. My father was hungry and child-like and accepted Jesus in his heart after asking how he could do so. My mother said, "This is nothing new. I know everything. I learned all about this in my Catechism class long ago." So we did not press the issue with her right then. We mentioned to her that head knowledge and heart knowledge were two different things. The greatest distance is between the head and the heart. We had to leave them and rush back for the afternoon sessions; but we continued to pray much for my mother and for all our relations.

At the end of the Convention, we were asked to pass the word around in Poona that an ex-film star would be coming there to share her testimony. She wanted others to know the miraculous changes in her life after she had asked Jesus to come into her heart as her Lord and Savior. She was a Muslim married to a Hindu, so she had been exposed to two different religions. She was a slave to smoking and used to smoke sixty cigarettes a day. She was able to get rid of this and other habits in her life with His help and grace. We returned to Poona and promptly sent the message around, informing people to bring a picnic lunch and come to Empress Gardens on January 26th 1977. It was a public holiday. Many agreed to come.

CHAPTER 27

We arrived at Empress Gardens and looked all over. There was not a soul in sight. None of the people we had informed came, nor did the actress! There was just one other lady Cathy,* who had come along with us. Absolutely strange! Or was it?

Since we had our picnic lunch, we decided to stay on and have a picnic. While we sat there and chatted, Cathy suddenly asked us about our Baptism. At first, we were taken aback as to how she knew about it. Then we realized the Anglican priest, who visited us on the day of our Baptism, must have been led to share the news with her. She was the teacher traveling with him that day.

As we spoke to her, there was such a change in her countenance. She longed to be baptized as well. We prayed very much about it and told her to search the Scriptures to be certain for herself. We did not want her to be influenced by our decision. Cathy read God's Word and she too was convicted and determined to obey the Lord. So that day was not really a waste after all. Cathy obeyed God and followed

Him through the waters of Baptism in the New Life Center.

Here again, we kept quiet about it, but then the Lord convicted us we were not to be His silent followers. We had to make it known, whatever the cost. Cathy informed her parents, who are Roman Catholics, and that is when the trouble started. People blamed us and could not understand why we had done this. There were arguments and bitterness in hearts. We were blacklisted. People looked down on us and detested us.

We felt it deeply when we knew people kept talking about us, and the priests forbade them to meet us. It was all the more hurtful when we heard that even our 'friends' had turned against us. They had forbidden their children to enter our home. It hurt the children and me, but it did not get us down completely. In fact, I can truly say, "The joy of the Lord is my strength."

It was tough no doubt, but through it all, we knew Jesus was with us, for He has said in His Word... *"Never will I leave you; never will I forsake you."* (Hebrews 13:5).

He has also said, *"I tell you whoever acknowledges Me before men, the Son of Man will also acknowledge him before the angels of God."* (Luke 12:8).

On the 21st February 1977, there was a weeklong seminar held at the New Life Center on the book of Zechariah. This prophet had a vision on the 24th day of the month. So on the very first day of the seminar, I said, "Lord, I want You to speak to me in a very specific way on the 24th of this month." I had no idea what He would say, but He knew!

On February 24th, the speaker told us how Jesus was building His Church in these last days with people from different religions and denominations. He is choosing people who are willing to separate themselves from the world and unto Him.

At the end of the meeting, he said there would be no altar call. Each of our places would be an altar where we could meet the Lord individually. I was deep in prayer and I said, "Lord, today is the 24th, the day I asked You to speak to me. Please Lord speak, I am listening." With my eyes closed, I could see the word 'SEPARATION' written in capital letters. "Separation from whom . . . from what . . . Lord?"

He then made it clear that I had to separate from the Roman Catholic Church. I could not place my feet in two separate boats. I knew obedience is better than sacrifice. I **had** to obey the Lord and make the break. I had to break away from my childhood religion, traditions, everything. It was a very, very difficult decision to make. But then I had said, "Speak Lord" and when He spoke I had to obey, no matter what the cost.

I do not claim that God speaks to everyone in the same way but He certainly spoke to me. I was able to obey Him, only with His grace and strength, because I knew I could not do this on my own. I told my children that this was a personal decision and I did not want them to follow blindly. The Lord had spoken to me as an individual. My son, however, had already been convicted of this, before I had. My two daughters continued attending the Catholic Church. After a fortnight, they knew they could not continue either and they also made a clean break. So by March 1977, all four of us had stopped attending the Roman Catholic Church.

From November 1976, people were praying that we would not leave the Church, when it had not even entered our minds to do so. Now four months later, the final decision was made by all four of us.

It was only at Easter, that our absence from the Catholic Church was noticed. A lady came over and asked me why we had stopped going to church. I told her we had never stopped attending church. In fact, we were now attending a Bible teaching Church and we were being richly fed with God's Word. Once news spread...and spread...the crisis took place. More and more people were warned not to speak to us nor meet us. They said we were a bad influence. Instead of feeling anger and bitterness in our hearts as news came back to us, the Lord just flooded our hearts with His 'agape love.' In fact, we prayed for the people who spoke ill of us.

Actually, I cannot blame them. I am sure I would have felt the same and done likewise if I were in their place. In the past, I would always fight up for my religion and traditions if anyone dared to talk about them. But now, it was all different. Once I decided to follow Jesus, there was just no turning back. I can truly sing these words and mean them with all my heart:

"Though no one joins me,
Still I will follow,

No turning back

No turning back."

Friends stopped being friends. People stopped coming over to our home. When we walked out of our gate, we were looked at with displeasure. Can you imagine what it felt like staying in a Co-operative Housing Society, yet not being a part of the Society at all?

Even though the people of St. Patrick's Town stopped talking to us, we prayed much for them. In fact, we claimed them for the Lord and His Kingdom. As we prayed for them, the Lord gave us a wonderful assurance from His Word, in Habakkuk 2: 2-3 *"Write down clearly on clay tablets what I reveal to you, so that it can be read at a glance. Put it in writing, because it is not yet time for it to come true. But the time is coming quickly, and what I show you will come true. It may seem slow in coming, but wait for it; it will certainly not be delayed."* (GNB).

I underlined these verses in my Bible and wrote 'St. Pat's Town, May 1977' next to it. We knew God would settle matters in His own good time. Till then we would pray.

The Lord's love and grace was more than sufficient for our every need. *"If God be for us, who can be against us?"* He brought people from outside our colony to visit us. I can hardly remember our home being empty even for a single day. Someone or the other belonging to the Family of God would drop in. Our days were full. There was no time to dwell on the hurt we might have felt because of the circumstances around us. People who needed prayers would come home and ask me to pray for them. I was just open to the Lord's leading and guiding. I was His available vessel and He filled me with His power and ability.

CHAPTER 28

The months flew by and we continued searching the Scriptures to learn more and more about God through His Word. Soon the year came to an end and we were in December 1977. It was going to be our first Christmas out of the Catholic Church. All my life, Christmas meant, besides the birth of Christ, new clothes, gifts and a variety of cakes and sweets made at home. With all the extra work to cope with, invariably tempers would fly. The message of Christmas seemed to lose its true meaning.

What would we do this year without Midnight Mass, which was so important to us? How would we ever feel it was Christmas without it? And what about returning home to find our gifts under the Christmas tree? I must admit I felt rather nostalgic and started crying. Then fortunately, I reached for God's Word and was astounded as I read what God had to say about keeping of feast days. In Amos 5:21-22, He says, *"I hate, I despise your religious feasts; I cannot stand your assemblies. Even though you bring me burnt offerings and grain offerings, I will not accept*

*them. Though you bring me choice fellowship offer-
ings, I will have no regard for them."*

When I recalled the first Christmas day, I felt the
Lord telling me, "This is not the way I want you to
celebrate Christmas." Jesus left His Heavenly throne
with all that splendor and majesty, to be born in real
poverty on earth. He had no new clothes, but was
wrapped in a swaddling cloth. He did not even have a
decent place to lay His head. He was born in a manger
with animals around Him. And how do we celebrate
Christmas? Many people have taken CHRIST out
of Christmas and more importance is laid on new
clothes, gifts and other festivities. People often
write, "Merry Xmas" making Christ the unknown
figure 'X..' Although we would go to Church on
Christmas day, that was nothing in comparison to all
the time spent on other preparations and expenses for
Christmas.

The New Life Center did not have a midnight
service for Christmas and I really longed for that. So
I asked the Lord to show me a place I could go and
worship with my family that Christmas. And He said,
"Why not here, in your home?" I replied, "Here Lord,
with whom?" And He brought to my mind the names
of three people whom I should contact. I decided to
contact them later. I rose from my bed and went to
the kitchen to make myself a cup of tea. Imagine my
surprise, at seeing one of the three people I was to
contact standing at my kitchen door. After he came in
and had tea with me, I asked him what he was doing
for Christmas. He replied that he was wondering
what to do and where to go.

I related to him my dialogue I had with the Lord minutes ago, and asked him to contact the other two people and find out their plans. We met and decided to assemble together at my home for a special time of praise and worship on Christmas Eve. As word went round, our numbers increased and nineteen of us gathered for a meaningful and precious time of fellowship together that night.

After the meeting, I was prompted to ask them if they would like to come the following week to meet at the Lord's feet. It would be good to thank Him for the past year and to commit the New Year into His hands. They agreed. So we assembled on New Year's Eve, and had a wonderful meeting. Since this was a Sunday and we had begun the year in this manner, I thought why not continue in the same way?

I asked those present if they would like to come and praise and worship the Lord together every Sunday. Thus began the "Sunday Evening Fellowship" at 79 St. Patrick's Town. The numbers fluctuated. At times there were just a few of us but later we had over seventy people gather in our home. God stretched our walls to accommodate all present. We had people from every tribe and nation present. We were one in the family of God as we praised and worshipped Him together. Here again, I was glad we had the Nursery room and furniture. It was ample to meet the needs of our growing fellowship.

To go back to Christmas day of 1977. The Lord worked out the spiritual side of it, but I would now like to dwell on the material side as well. I was very, very low on funds. In fact, I had absolutely nothing to spend. Formerly, if I did not have money, I would go ahead and buy things on credit. Especially at Christmas I would run up bills. But this time, the Lord made it very clear to me that this was unnecessary.

I tried to compromise and thought if I did not make all the sweets and cakes, at least I could make a few Rose a Coquese. For years I had made them really well, however, when I tried to compromise this time and mixed the batter, everything seemed to go wrong. I went on thickening, then thinning, thickening and thinning over and over again...but all to no avail.

At last I got the message from my patient Lord and Master that I was **not** to make anything at all. Well! What happened to all the batter? We had pancakes morning, noon and night! I must say we had never tasted such delicious pancakes before! What a wonderful Father we have. He really knows how to discipline His children.

On Christmas morning, my neighbor Viola came to wish us. As she was leaving, she asked us to come over for lunch. Relations were improving among the neighbors once again! It was good to know that we were accepted by some of them. I was really touched by her invitation. I hugged her and started crying. She wondered why. How could I tell her we had nothing special for lunch that day? I just said, "Jesus loves us too much. He really cares for us." We had a really sumptuous lunch with lobster, chicken, pork, steaming pillau and fresh vegetables...rounded off with Nobby's famous Christmas cake, moist and rich and full of raisins and nuts. Wow! What a meal!

*" So do not worry, saying, 'What shall we eat?'
or 'What shall we drink?' or 'What shall we wear?'
For the pagans run after all these things, and your
Heavenly Father knows that you need them. But seek
first His kingdom and His righteousness, and all
these things will be given to you as well."* (Matthew
6: 31-33)

Our Father God is so true to His promises. If only
we can trust Him with all our heart.

We could not stop thanking God for His provision. On returning home, we had a phone call from a
friend near Bund Garden. She asked if I would come
to her flat in the evening to conduct a prayer meeting.
She told me to bring our dinner along. Whoever heard
of a prayer meeting on Christmas evening before? It
was either spent in merry making, visiting friends or
people coming over to share the Christmas goodies.
But a prayer meeting? Unheard of !

This was one Christmas where I had to forget
about long-held customs and traditions. I agreed to
the meeting but said we would not bring our dinner.
How could I tell her we had not cooked any? She
insisted that we stay on for dinner after the meeting.
She had invited a few people from her neighborhood.
We had a wonderful time of praise and worship. After
having our spiritual food, we had food for our bodies.
There was tasty biryani prepared. So much was left
over, that my friend packed some for us to have the
following day.

Two days after Christmas, the postman arrived
with not one but two money orders! How I thanked
and praised God for the lesson He taught me so

lovingly and in such a gentle but firm way. Actually, this money had to arrive for Christmas but somehow, somewhere, it got delayed. This I know was due to divine intervention. If I had received the money earlier, I am positive I would have gone ahead with some of my past traditions. But the Lord wanted to teach me a lesson and let me know the true meaning of Christmas. So He allowed this delay. Yet He saw to it that we did not starve or go hungry. Different people provided for our meals. What a loving and caring Father we have. He knows every single thing about us His children.

The following year I had enough money on Christmas day but I had learned my lesson from my Lord and Master on how to fix my priorities during this season. Surely His rod and staff are there to guide and discipline us.

I do very much believe in Christmas and what it cost Jesus to be born as a human being, but Jesus has shown me the 'extra frills' are not really necessary. There is more to life than all these celebrations. What is important is to remember to keep CHRIST in Christmas and to give Him first place. We can truly do this, when we allow Christ to be the Lord and Savior of our hearts, our lives and our homes.

CHAPTER 29

During the annual convention of October 1976, one of the talks was on fasting. Jesus had said to His disciples, *"When* you fast" and not *"If* you fast."* The preacher drew this to our attention. Jesus expects us to fast. This was too much for a new believer. I said to myself, "My brother, this maybe for you, but it is certainly not for me." I could not even give up one meal!

Now we flip over a couple of years and it is October 1978. We are attending another convention. An announcement was made that many of those attending the convention had decided to fast for three days and nights to pray for our nation. I had a strong feeling that the Lord was urging me to fast the entire week of the convention. I did not question or murmur this time. I knew this was from the Lord. So I obeyed and fasted. I, who could not give up one meal, was willing to fast the entire week. *"His grace is sufficient for every need."*

Each day I would rise early to prepare breakfast and lunch for the rest of the family. The whole morning was spent in church. I would drive the children home for lunch and then back again for the afternoon and evening sessions. It was remarkable the strength the Lord gave me. Surely I could say, *"Man does not live by bread alone, but by every word that comes from the mouth of God."* I did not feel hungry. Neither did I have the urge to eat, even though I was cooking.

A map of India was placed on the floor and all of us would kneel around it and literally cry to the Lord to save our nation.

Soon after the Convention, the "International Singing Team" came to Poona. They were a dedicated group who left everything to follow Jesus. They lived entirely by faith, not knowing where their next meal would come from. Yet Jesus always provided the essentials for them. Praise His wonderful Name.

From Poona they proceeded to Miraj. At this time, my daughter Cheryl had given up her secretarial post and so accompanied them for a fortnight. Patty my younger daughter had gone to the Bible Center to attend a Scripture Union Leaders' Retreat. There was just Robin and myself at home. As we were preparing to go to church that Sunday morning, Robin found he had enough money in his savings box to invite me for lunch. We were quite excited deciding where we should go for our treat. By the time we reached church, we still had not made up our minds.

While I was taking my Sunday school class, I missed a part of the sermon. On re-entering the church, I realized the sermon had been on 'Fasting.' Pastor Timothy John was going over the points again.

He mentioned:

A 3-day fast,

A 7-day fast,

A 21-day fast and

A 40-day fast.

With each fast, he gave examples from the Bible. As he dwelt on the last fast, the Lord said, "That is for you."

"Me Lord? Forty days? Impossible!"

But it was clear He wanted me to go through with it. Well, I thought, if this is from the Lord, He would surely give me the grace and strength to cope. I knew that in my own strength a forty-day fast was next to impossible.

How could I tell Robin about breaking our lunch date? I came out of church and asked him where he had decided to go for lunch. He said it was up to me.

"Son, if I dare go for lunch, I am afraid the food will stick in my throat."

"What has happened mum? Why have you changed your mind so suddenly?"

I told him that the Lord wanted me to fast and I added, "Only the Lord can help me do it my son." My beloved son said, "It's alright Mum, I also will not eat today. Let us go home and pray together and wait on the Lord."

What plans we had made on our way to church! Now they had completely changed. *"We can make our plans, but the final outcome is in God's hands."* (We find this written in Proverbs 16:1 T. L.B.) We came home and knelt together and prayed. We were in such close communion with God and with each other. The Lord made it very clear why He wanted me to fast. He gave me a number of points to intercede for and these words came out so vividly and clearly to me from 2 Chronicles 7: 14 *"If My people, who are called by My Name, will humble themselves and pray and seek My face and turn from their wicked ways, then will I hear from Heaven and will forgive their sin and will heal their land."*

It was such a precious time together - Mother and son interceding at the Throne of Grace for our family, our nation and for ourselves.

CHAPTER 30

Birthdays came and went, Christmas and New Year too. What remarkable strength the Lord gave me. I cooked for my children. I carried on teaching and yet, I did not have the urge to eat during those forty days. I am not saying this to get any applause because I could never have done this on my own. I know for certain the Lord chose me at that particular time for a specific purpose. All God wants is our availability, and He gives us the ability to fulfill His plans. It was a very special time for me, as I spent a long, long time alone in the presence of my Lord and Master.

Cheryl had returned from Miraj, as she had received a letter from St. Mary's Teachers' Training College summoning her for an interview. She had now decided she would like to become a Teacher. She was successful in the interview and underwent her training, which lasted for two years. When she completed her training, she thoroughly enjoyed herself teaching in St. Paul's Nursery School.

Robin and Patricia joined Wadia College and were great witnesses. While in college, Robin tried various doors, but everywhere he turned, the doors would shut in his face. Without Jesus in his life, he could have been so disappointed and frustrated; but knowing that Jesus has the best for us, Robin was able to accept this as God's will. He then helped as a volunteer worker with Scripture Union. This was the first time he had left home for any length of time. We three girls really felt his absence immensely. The Lord was preparing us, however, for longer separations later on.

After Patricia completed her B. A. at Wadia College, she joined the Poona University to study for her M.A. in Psychology. I do not know how she was able to study and concentrate with all the comings and goings in our home. Yet Patricia is an excellent example of what a Christian student should be. She knew how to set her priorities right. Daily she would diligently work, so that even when a crisis arose during her examination, there was no panic. Nobody was aware when it was examination time for Patty. She never absented herself from any of our prayer and fellowship meetings. Never did she make an excuse, "I cannot come for the meeting, as I have to study for my exams." In fact, she was faithful in whatever she set out to do. She knew where her strength would come from. She honored God and He honored her.

"The fear of the Lord is the beginning of wisdom." (Psalm 111: 10) While Robin was working with Scripture Union, he felt the Lord would have him enter full-time ministry. He wanted to join a

Bible College. Where could he go? He thought of enquiring in a few colleges in India. Even before he made enquiries, the door to Singapore Bible College opened wide for him. This was because of Paul Tan from Singapore. He was working with Operation Mobilization and met us through Henry D'Souza, a common friend, who later became my son in law.

Paul was used as God's instrument to pave the way for Robin's admission to the Bible College. It was also through Paul that the Faith Methodist Church in Singapore very kindly sponsored Robin and consented to support him financially. We just had to pay Robin's airfare. We knew if this was the Lord's Will, we would collect the fare, and get it we did. Truly, He gives us much more than we ever dream of or dare to ask Him. Such a great and mighty God we have as our Heavenly Father.

Robin was the first Indian from India to join this college. He flew out in June 1983. It was tough being away from home and adjusting to a new culture. But the Lord was in complete control and saw him through. What is more, He filled Robin with His wisdom and understanding. Praise God! Lonely as we were without him, the Lord filled us with His peace. Truly, His grace is sufficient for every need.

CHAPTER 31

My father went to be with the Lord in May 1983 after a brief illness. He really loved Jesus and used to sit daily at His feet reading from His Word. I can still recall the many discussions we used to have together about the Lord. Dad was so open to learning more. Age was no barrier. He realized that being religious was not the answer. There was much more to it.

My prayer is that every member of my family will be open and obedient to God's Word. I pray they will come to know Jesus as Lord and Savior in a personal way. May the Holy Spirit work in each one's life and heart. I pray they will realize it is not at all sufficient just being born in a Christian family.

I know for certain now, that religion is definitely no ticket to heaven. What is essential, as Jesus said to Nicodemus, a religious leader in John 3, is to be **born again**, born of the Spirit into God's family. We should believe there is nobody else and no other way to the Father but through Jesus. Jesus said, "*I am* *the way, the truth and the life. No one comes to the Father except through Me."* (John 14: 6)

Mum's heart softened some time after Dad's death. She was now prepared to hear what we had to share with her. She realized that head knowledge was not enough. She repented of her sins and with childlike simplicity and trust asked Jesus into her heart. How we rejoiced. Praise the Lord. He makes all things beautiful in His Time!

"Have Thine own way Lord, Have Thine own way."

Yes, our Master Potter surely knows how to mould us and make us into what He wants us to be, if only we yield ourselves and every area of our lives to Him.

In May 1978, we attended the First Missionary Conference held in Poona. We were so touched by the end of it, that we were all set to leave everything and join as Missionaries. Rev. Chandapilla the Speaker, however, told me that my mission field was right where God had placed me. I still had the responsibility of looking after my three children.

How often we feel we want to go out to some distant place and work for the Lord. But the greatest test is to work for Him and witness for Him just where He has placed us. It is a real test to practice what we preach with our family and friends...with our neighbors and with those we rub shoulders with daily. I did not realize it then, but God chose my family and me to be witnesses right in St. Patrick's Town.

Noel my brother, used to pay us monthly visits from Bombay. He would watch us closely. If we said or did anything we should not be doing or saying, he would say, "Oh! Is this the way you are supposed to be Christians?"

It was tough! We were being watched all the time. This made us realize our commitment was not only in word. Our deeds had to prove it. No more gossiping or unkind words. No more criticism or bad language. It was tough. We either had to live in the flesh or in the Spirit. We had to ask the Spirit of God to help us daily. What is more, He still helps us. We are far from perfect, but He still fills us with grace and strength to be more and more like Him. We need to continually ask Him for a refilling.

In school, I would spend the first part of the morning teaching the Nursery children about God's love. We used to sing choruses together and pray, followed by me telling them Bible stories. As the day proceeded, the children's noisy and troublesome behavior would cause me to lose my temper and shout at them. Suddenly, God's Spirit would convict me. Was *this* the same person teaching about God's love in the morning? I learned that I could discipline them without getting mad at them. This was certainly not self-taught. I was going through the Divine School of Learning. I am still learning many lessons at my Master's feet. I am so weak and I need constant help and guidance from God's Spirit to mould me and change me into what He wants me to be.

Circumstances led me to wonder whether I should continue running my Nursery. I was very hurt and depressed over certain situations. I did not want my feelings to get the better of me so I took it to the

Lord in prayer. I told Him I was willing to close my Nursery if it was His Will. It was wonderful having the Nursery at home. The timings were convenient... from nine in the morning to noon. I was my own boss and respected by the school children and their parents. Yet, if it was God's Will, I was willing to give it up and surrender it completely to Him.

When there was total surrender from my part, the Lord showed me it was still very much His Will for me to continue "Happy Hours." He did this by sending me new admissions daily without me even advertising. I had over fifty pupils and had to stop new admissions. Praise God, we can take any and every problem to Him. He really cares for us. He gives us so much peace as He solves our problems.

"Cast all your burdens on Him because He cares for you." (1 Peter 5: 7)

Trying to pay my bills regularly has always been a thorn in my flesh. The bills used to keep mounting. In December 1981, I said, "Lord, will You please send me money from somewhere to pay my bills? I have so many bills to pay Lord."

Prompt came the reply, "Sell your car."

"Oh Lord, I need money and You tell me to sell my car."

I always wanted to keep my 'Black Beauty' for sentimental reasons, and here, I was told by the Lord to sell my car in order to pay my bills. I told the Lord if He really wanted me to sell the car to show me by sending a buyer who would offer me a good price for it. *"Ask and you shall receive."*

I did not advertise. I did not make a noise about it as people made such fun of my car. They told me she was fit for a Museum. The Lord, however, sent me a customer promptly, too promptly in fact! This man came over and was ready to buy her there and then. He even had the cash in his hand. Talk of me being sentimental, Cheryl beat me. She just did not want me to sell the car. I knew this was a definite order from the Lord, so I hardened my heart and finalized the transaction.

I would not even go out to see her being driven out for the last time. The parting was too much to bear. Tears streamed down our cheeks as 'Black Beauty' went out of our lives and home forever. I had her for twenty-five years. She had become such a part of us . . . but the Master Gardener was doing much pruning in my life. He kept teaching me new lessons. 'Letting go' was a part of my training. And a good thing too, because we only see the 'here and now' but God was aware what was going to happen to me in the very near future.

'Black Beauty' went, and I was able to pay all my bills. Praise God for the way He leads us and guides us; for the way He prunes us and corrects us. Like a Master Gardener, He removes all unwanted things in our lives. I learned more and more that I could not hold on to earthly possessions.

I discovered this even in my personal life, with habits and unobserved sins, which could eat into me like a cancer. Our precious Lord and Master dealt with me with such love but yet very firmly. He is still working in me and making me what He wants me to be.

CHAPTER 32

It is not enough to learn all these lessons and keep them to ourselves. We must let God's light shine through our lives to others and tell them about Him. After one of the Scripture Union Camps I was led to minister to the girls at Saint Helena's School. I paid weekly visits to this school to share God's Word with them. As I ministered to those girls who were on fire for the Lord, they in turn were an encouragement to me. Come rain or storm, I looked forward to my weekly visits to their school.

Then one fine day, most unexpectedly I received a phone call from Mrs. Enid Salins who was the wife of the Air Force Station Commander. She had heard about our prayer meetings at home and wanted me to start similar meetings in her home. She mentioned that Percy and her husband Godfrey had been together at the Air Force Academy at Begumpet, Secunderabad. It made me think for a moment, 'If Percy were alive, he too would have been an Air Vice Marshal and the Station Commander somewhere perhaps!'

As her plea came across the phone, I had to collect my thoughts once again. I told her I was unable to come straightaway but would certainly come as soon as I was able. I kept praying and waiting on the Lord for His perfect timing even in this. I first paid the Salins a social visit with Robin during the Christmas vacation. They gave us such a warm welcome and insisted we stay for lunch. Rank and position meant nothing to them. They were so humble and friendly. We immediately felt at home with them.

The next time I visited them I shared the Gospel message with Enid and her daughter Shama. I had a booklet 'Journey through Life' which is used by Scripture Union. It gave them much food for thought. I told them that religion and good works are not everything. We need salvation. We need to have a personal relationship with Jesus and ask His forgiveness. Then we need to ask Him to come into our hearts as Lord and Savior.

They listened and hungered for more. They wanted their friends to come and hear the Good News of Salvation as well. They invited others to attend. As Godfrey was the big boss of the Station, many people fought shy of attending these meetings in his home. We knew, however, that the Lord would bring those He wanted to attend. We had five families who were keen to come for the meetings. We commenced with fortnightly meetings, but soon they requested me to come weekly. Since they were so hungry for God's Word, I agreed to visit them for a weekly Bible Study.

With my bag slung on my shoulder, filled with songbooks and my Bible, I would take a rickshaw to East Street and then wait for the Air Force bus. It was a long, long drive. Come sun, or rain the Lord gave me the strength and desire to carry on. I taught them new songs. They learned to pray spontaneously. We followed the Navigators' Course whereby the group learned more of "Who Jesus is" and "What Jesus Requires of Me." Despite their heavy schedules, they still attempted the assignments set each week. It was a joy going there and seeing how hungry they were. Sometimes I would take members from our Fellowship at home to enact skits with messages for them. God was using us in different ways to share His love and Good News. It was really worth the time and effort. It was rewarding.

A few months later, the entire Salins family realized that each of them had to die to themselves and allow Jesus to live in and through them. They repented of their sins and asked Jesus to come into their hearts as Lord and Savior. Together one evening, right in their own garden, Godfrey, Enid, Rohan and Shama who was then eight months pregnant, were baptized through immersion. Alleluia! What rejoicing there was! I was overjoyed at having obeyed the Lord in going to their home for these meetings.

A friendship had developed between the Salins and me. Enid had an elderly aunt staying with her. She desired to go to Chandigarh and needed someone to accompany her, as she was unable to walk on her own. She moved with the help of a 'walker.' They requested me to accompany their aunt to Chandigarh, where Enid's sister would meet her. Our train was due to arrive in the wee hours of the morning. Being nervous we would oversleep, aunty told me not to latch our compartment door. The conductor had been given orders by her to wake us in time. I did not feel very happy or safe about this arrangement, but I listened to her.

I read Psalm 91 before we retired for the night, and believed that Almighty God would keep us safe and secure.

Suddenly, in the middle of the night, I was rudely awakened as the train steamed into a station. Hundreds of feet came charging down the platform and you could hear shouts like battle cries. Before the train halted, crowds of unruly terrorists entered our compartment. Like a shot, I stretched out and quickly bolted our door. They banged and banged on each door so savagely demanding to enter.

The two of us hugged on to each other and called to our Father in Heaven. We knew He was much mightier and powerful than all these terrorists put together. We continued to pray and beseeched God to protect us. What if . . .what if . . . the door was not bolted when these terrorists entered? I dread to imagine what would have been our fate. Age would not have meant a thing to these wild men. Praise God, before we reached our destination, God made it possible for these men to alight from the train. It was a horrendous experience, but again, I felt the near-ness and loving care of our Savior. I read Psalm 91 again. Verse 15 says *"When he calls on Me, I will answer; I will be with him in trouble, and rescue him and honor him."* And He certainly did!

The Salins families have grown in grace and strength. They are being used mightily by the Lord in Secunderabad where they have settled down after retirement.

God wants us to study His Word and share it with others, so that they in turn will teach the same to others.

CHAPTER 33

The summer holidays of 1984 had begun. I sing-songed to myself, as the last 'Happy Hours' pupil skipped out of the front door. I could not wait another minute to convert the schoolroom into our sitting room. This pushing and lifting of school chairs, tables and cupboards, the moving and arranging of our sitting room furniture and the final stacking of school material was routine. We did it twice a year, every year.

"I can do this alone," I thought, not wanting to wait until Cheryl and Patty eventually returned home.

"Not bad," I panted to myself as I wiped the stream of perspiration off my cheek and looked at the near empty schoolroom. "Just that big old cupboard left," I breathed deeply, as I caught a minute under the fan to cool off a bit.

The cupboard was big and heavy, but I got behind it like a pro packer and mover. Heave ho! I was panting. Heave ho! Ah, it had tilted a little. Good! It was moving. I was panting harder, pushing harder.

Heaving, pressing all my weight against it. Straighten my arms, push! Again... And again... And again... To the left... To the right... Back a little more... My whole body was hot. The sweat poured down my head, my arms and legs. And my back...it felt sore. "Just one last push...Huuuuuuuuuh!"

I fell on the floor exhausted. My body ached all over. My back was killing me. Unable to move, I shut my eyes wearily and fell asleep on the floor.

The next day, I did not give the pain a second thought, but carried on with my normal chores. Time and again, I would get terrible burning pain shooting down my leg and up my spine. I paid no attention and thought it was a muscle strain. I had no idea that any serious damage had been done.

Suddenly, one Sunday evening in July, as I was preparing the room for our prayer meeting, I got a terrible catch in my back. "AAAaaa!" I screamed with pain. For some time, I could not sit nor could I lie down. In fact, I could not move at all. It was unbearable. The pain persisted over the next few days. It grew worse when I got into certain positions. I went to the Military Hospital for a thorough examination. I was advised complete rest for ten days with pain-killers and Calmpose thrice daily. I thought this was too much rest and treatment for a muscular catch. So when the pain eased with the medication after a few days, I did not continue it for the entire period and neither did I rest any longer.

I carried on with my teaching, housework and my meetings at St Helena's and the Air Force Station. I pushed myself, in spite of the discomfort and the erratic pain. At times I could even hear the grating sound of the vertebrae as the edges were giving way.

X-rays were taken. There was something radically wrong with my spine. The Adviser in Orthopedics at the Military Hospital told me to get a spinal brace made from the Artificial Limb Center. He said that I would have to wear this all my life and what is more, I would have to learn to live with the pain. As time went on, however, the pain grew worse and there were more alarming symptoms. There were traces of me beginning to lose control.

Mitzi my friend was now posted in Calcutta. It was fortunate how the Lord brought her to Poona just at the correct time. She had spent her annual leave in the South and decided to pay us a visit on her way back to Calcutta. When she arrived, she was surprised to see me carrying on in spite of my pain and other symptoms. Having worked in the Orthopedic Center at Kirkee, she knew the correct people to contact. She took me to Kirkee where I had a fresh set of X-rays taken. They diagnosed it as Spondylolisthesis, a real mouthful, what ever that might mean. Mitzi explained that my spine was in a very serious condition and I had to be extremely careful the rest of my life. It had shifted! It could damage the spinal cord.

As I lay down that afternoon, trying to gather my thoughts, I wondered what should I do now. I thought of my meetings at St.Helena's and the Air Force Station. I knew I would not be able to continue my Bible Studies with them any longer. But I still wanted to work and be used by the Lord. I said, "Lord, You are aware of what has happened to me. I am going to be housebound for the rest of my life. What will You have me do?" This time I did not ask "Why?"

The reply came clearly, "WRITE A BOOK." Amazed I asked, "**Me**? Write a book? I'm no writer, I am only a Kindergarten teacher." And again the command came very clearly "WRITE A BOOK."

Many years had passed, since I had wanted to write a book but I had never got down to it. All this time the Lord had patiently waited to see whether I would keep my word. But now in 1984, He reminded me of my desire to write a book in 1969 after my three accidents. By writing a book I could reach out to many more people under the Lord's anointing instead of just a few people in limited places. I recalled His command to me after I received the Baptism of the Spirit, "Go tell the world..." Did all this have any connection? Only time will tell.

Before Mitzi's leave expired, she took me to a neuro-surgeon, Colonel Biswas, better known as Sandy. After examining me and seeing my X-rays, he laid the cards on the table. I was so much at ease and peace with him. He told me there was no way out; I had to have an operation soon. I would have liked it postponed till after Robin's Christmas vacation, so that I could prepare his favorite dishes while he was at home. But the signs and symptoms grew worse. We knew the operation had to be performed immediately.

I did not want to alarm Robin and ask him to come home from Singapore. It would have hampered his studies. Yet, I longed for him to be with us. Even though I was not completely frank with Robin, he read between the lines of my letters. He had a feeling that things were worse than I had made them out to be. So he approached the Principal and put him in the picture.

By mid-September, tension was mounting at home among us three girls! We had no idea what to expect and what the outcome of this operation would be. Each time we looked at one another, it was a battle to keep the tears hidden.

Thoughts churned in my mind. Would I come out of this operation alive? What would happen to my children? What about the unpaid bills in my cupboard? Where would I get money for those bills and for the operation?

"O you of little faith, why do you doubt Me? Why can't you trust Me?" How it must grieve our Father to see us weak children never taking Him at His Word. "Oh Lord, increase my faith."

There were some practical issues to be seen to before going to hospital. I asked some friends to help me write my Will. I enquired at the Society office if my house papers were in order so that there would be no trouble for the children if anything happened to me.

But the bills! How could I tell the children about the bills that kept coming? There was the water bill, electricity bill, and telephone bill. I phoned the bank and found I had exactly Rs.110/- in my account. What a strange coincidence! Percy had the same amount in his bank account when he crashed! But that money bought so little now. What would I do? Nay! What would my children do if I went? How would they manage?

I realized that we do not need great faith. What we need is to have childlike faith and trust in a great and faithful God. Why should we worry about our food and clothes and unpaid bills? Jesus tells us if He cares for the flowers that are here today and gone tomorrow, if He cares for the birds, then how much **more** does He care for us.

"Yes Lord, I believe that... BUT."

Can't we say "Yes Lord" and believe? No! We have to add a hundred BUTS after it.

"What do you want for your birthday Mum?" Immediately would come the reply, "Money." Every time Cheryl and Patty asked me this question, I would give them the same reply. I knew exactly why I wanted the money . . . to pay my bills. Since I had a strong premonition I would not return home, what was the need to ask for anything else?

CHAPTER 34

I went to the extent of phoning the Salins at the Air Force Station and I made them promise that they would see to all formalities and expenses of my funeral. They were shocked and asked me what happened to my faith. I told them I was just being practical. I wanted to see to all these details before I went to hospital. Can you imagine me doing all these things quietly without telling my daughters? I could not tell Cheryl about this, as she used to break down too often those days.

Since Patty was the stronger of the two, I decided to inform her of what I had done. She listened very bravely, but that night, while we were praying, she broke down and said, "Mama, you think I am stronger, because I do not show what I feel." That was enough for us. The three of us hugged each other and nothing could stop us sobbing. How would we face the days ahead? We knew we needed someone of our own to be a source of strength to us. All three of us longed for Robin, but we would not dare call him away from his studies and his college.

Just a few days before I was to be admitted, we received a letter from Robin mentioning that the Principal would allow him to take a term off if it was essential for him to come home. He could make up this term later at the end of his course. That was enough for us! As long as he would not miss a whole year! I did not need a second letter from him. Immediately I rang International Booking and booked a call to Robin. I told him we had just received his letter and needed him as soon as he could possibly come. That was on Thursday 20th September 1984. He had not even enough money for his fare. The Lord, however, was in perfect control.

Friends and classmates rallied round him in his time of need and helped him. He not only got enough money for his fare but also something towards my hospital expenses. How absolutely thrilling it is to belong to the Family of God. I had not met his classmates and yet, we were one family bound together in Christ's love. All because of what Jesus had done for us at Calvary.

While Robin's needs were being met in Singapore, the Lord, the owner of the 'cattle on a thousand hills' was meeting our needs in Poona. The mother of one of my pupils asked me if I needed any help. Being such a general question, I said I would inform her if I needed any. Then very frankly, she asked, "Do you have enough money?" My face must have given me away, because she asked me again. I told her that I would ask my brother to give me my birthday gift in advance to use towards my hospital expenses.

She did not say anything further and went home. In a short while, I was surprised to see her return. She told me her husband mentioned that it was not enough to pray for people, she should **do** something also. She gave me a generous amount. I felt I could not possibly take it from her. Then this kind lady added, "If it is not enough, I will go home and get some more." I was so touched with her generosity, I cried and cried. I told her I could not accept this from her but she insisted. I thanked her very much. I thanked my Father in Heaven for speaking to her and I thanked her for being so prompt in obeying His voice.

That was only the beginning of what the Lord had in store for us. From that day on, we kept receiving money orders and cheques from various people as soon as they heard I had to undergo a spinal operation. There was I worrying and wondering what would happen to my children if anything happened to me. I was soon to learn that they were more **His** children than they were mine. I had only been His caretaker all these years. He showed me that ALL POWER is in His hands and we could rely on Him for **all** our needs.

I praised Him and thanked Him that He had shielded me and protected me all these years, enabling me to care for my children when they needed me. I praised Him that nothing happened to me when they were so young and depended on me. Now I was ready to hand over charge back to Him.

These verses had new meaning in my life now. *"Whoever finds his life will lose it, and whoever loses his life for My sake shall find it."* (Matthew 10: 39)

"Unless a kernel of wheat falls to the ground and dies, it remains only a single seed. But if it dies it produces many seeds." (John 12: 24)

There and then I rededicated my life, my children, my operation, my all to Him, knowing that was the best possible thing to do. Once I had done this, indescribable peace flooded my soul.

I was ready to go to hospital; only Robin had to arrive. Very early on Sunday 23rd September, he came and whistled our code at the bedroom window. He did not really know what to expect. I jumped out of bed, forgetting the seriousness of my back. I quickly went to open the door for him. What a homecoming! Tears of joy and sorrow intermingled. It was wonderful to have him home again. While having my Quiet Time that morning, I read Psalm 118 and was taken aback at the cry of victory in that Psalm. My eyes fell on a couple of verses again and again. I said, "Lord what are You trying to tell me?" Simultaneously, Cheryl was having her Quiet Time in another room. She came later and told me she was reading a beautiful Psalm and the Lord had spoken to her through it. On comparing notes, we found we had been reading the same verses at the same time! The Lord had spoken to both of us. What a tremendous confirmation!

Psalm 118:17 reads *"I will not die but live, and will proclaim what the Lord has done."* And Psalm119: 49-50 says, *" Remember Your word to Your servant, for You have given me hope. My comfort in my suffering is this: Your promise preserves my life."*

What more did I want? I took these promises and claimed them. I believed I was going to come through this operation successfully. After the operation I would proclaim far and wide all that the Lord had done for me. I received His promise and I believed it. I praised and thanked God for His promise given to me from His Word. We had a beautiful time of worship together as a family that morning, since I could not go to church.

The next day, I got ready to leave for the hospital. There was no fear at all. It was just as if I was going on a trip. All the preliminaries for my admission were completed. I was placed in Room No.6 with an Afghan lady, Nazbhow. I was able to share much about Jesus with her during my stay in hospital. We even managed to get her a Bible in her language later.

I celebrated my birthday two days before my operation. From early morning, I was flooded with love, flowers, cards and gifts. So many people came to visit me that day. Eventually in the evening the sister-in-charge, had to ask my visitors to leave, as it had been an extremely tiring day for me. Many forgot they were in a hospital. They thought they were visiting me back at 79 St.Patrick's Town!

CHAPTER 35

When I had phoned Mitzi in Calcutta, to inform her about my operation, she regretted that she would be unable to come to Poona. So I was pleasantly surprised to see her walk into my room very early on the 28th morning. Somehow, she had managed to get leave.

September 29th 1984 dawned. I was up bright and early to have my Quiet Time with the Lord. The nurse entered to prepare me for the operation. Mitzi then came, followed by my three beloved children. We had a beautiful time of praise and worship together. We committed one another to Him. Anyone walking in would never have imagined that in minutes the ambulance would arrive to take me to the Operation Theatre for major surgery. Praise God for the way He flooded us with His peace. We had direct access to His Throne Room. *"My peace I give unto you."* Yes, even in the midst of our storms, He can flood us with His peace . . .His peace that passeth all understanding.

The ambulance arrived and we went together to the Operation Theatre. We wished one another bravely. I knew the same Lord who was going along with me, would be with my children, strengthening them and blessing them with His peace throughout the day and the days ahead.

I was given an injection to calm me, but there was so much of movement and chatter in the corridor, it was difficult to be calm. I asked Mitzi to read some Psalms to me. I just wanted my heart and mind fixed on Jesus and on Him alone.

Psalm 23:4 *"Though I walk through the valley of the shadow of death, I will fear no evil, for You are with me."*

Psalm 121:1 *"I lift up my eyes to the hills where does my help come from? My help comes from the Lord, the Maker of heaven and earth."*

Psalm 91: 2 *" He is my refuge and my fortress, my God, in whom I trust."*

I cherished all these precious psalms in my heart. I lay with my eyes closed and hands joined, meditating on all I heard.

Colonel Biswas came in and asked me "What has happened? Are you frightened? Sleeping? Or praying?"

I told him I was praying. I knew the doctors would be standing there to perform the operation, but actually, the Greatest Physician would be present to guide them along. The trolley was wheeled to my bed to take me into the Theatre. God kept me at peace. As I was being wheeled in, I kept repeating, *"Though I walk through the valley of the shadow of death, I will fear no evil."*

Before I knew anything, the oxygen mask was being removed. The first thing I did was to wiggle my toes. As soon as I saw that both my feet could move and that I was not paralyzed, I said, "Praise the Lord," with such a thick tongue. I could hear them saying, "She's talking, she's talking."

And I could hear Colonel Biswas telling them that I was saying, "Praise the Lord."

I was glad that my last thoughts before the operation and my first thoughts after it were on my Lord. I could truly feel His presence in such an intimate way.

I was on my hospital bed for two whole months. It was a real time of testing as I lay on my bed and could not get out of it at all. The Lord taught me many a lesson there. As time passed, I began feeling depressed and frustrated. Self-pity started creeping in and got a real hold of me.

I worried about how the children were doing at home; what were they eating, their safety as they rushed up and down to hospital. The worries escalated as I heard of the assassination of Indira Gandhi our Prime Minister and the political upheaval, which followed. But what could I do? I was helpless and confined to bed. I learned to trust God all the more. He taught me countless lessons on my hospital bed.

In His perfect time, the Lord gave me good reading material to uplift me and teach me. Pastor Timothy John gave me "Hind's Feet on High Places." I could literally see myself portrayed in this book. What a wonderful Gardener we have. He continues to prune all the unwanted branches in our lives. I praise Him for the way He corrects us and moulds us into what He wants us to be.

During my stay in hospital, I was very much indebted to my children and a few friends who went out of their way to do everything for me. Many of my old friends from the colony had befriended us again and were of immense help. All wounds were healed. The Lord took care of my three gems and gave them the strength to cope with housework, the Nursery school and also with daily visits to the hospital. They saw to my every need. God bless my darlings.

I came home by the end of November. Here again, there was much adjustment required. Now I was no longer in charge or in control at home. The Lord taught me a lesson in humility. I had to depend on my children and others for every single detail. There was **nothing** I could do for myself. After being such an independent person all these years, overnight it had all changed. Things had to be done for me instead. I could not even walk without help. Lydia my phys-iotherapist, together with my children taught me to stand, to sit and to take my first steps again. I realized how much I had taken for granted formerly. I praised and thanked God the first time I sat on a chair. I had never dreamt of thanking Him for 'sitting' before.

Although I was very happy to be home with my loved ones, I would experience bouts of depression. "If only I could do this...if only I could do that." How often I would think and repeat these words over and over. One day I asked, "Lord, how much longer do

I have to be like this? When will I be normal again? I want to do something for You. What will You have me do?" And again the command was so clearly given, "WRITE THE BOOK."

As I lay in bed day after day, I would write in snatches and then place the book down again. I knew, however, that the Lord wanted me to complete this book and He was giving me the time to do so. I had to ask many people to uplift me in prayer as I collected my thoughts together to write.

As scheduled, I went to the hospital in January 1985, for a check- up and for X-rays to be taken. The results showed that the bone graft had been absorbed in the body. My condition was worse. What could be the reason? I was told to be extremely careful. "Don't do this and don't do that..."

"Why Lord, why?"

The Lord's reply shook me. "Remember you said, "Thy will be done" before your operation. Well it is still My will." I recalled the words of a song I had read before my operation, which I had made my prayer.

"Don't take my cross away.
My burdens keep humble
And teach me to pray.
If I murmur or grumble,
Give me strength to carry
My load day by day.
But don't take my burdens,
Or my cross away.

For I would grow careless
And idle I fear,
My eyes would be dry
And I would never shed a tear.
Lest I forget that
I need You each day,
Don't take my burdens,
Or my cross away."

If I meant those words, then God was complying with that prayer. Who could question any further? I longed to be active; to do things like I did before, but it was impossible. Quite often there were warning signals and I would have to stop and rest.

Many new shops had opened on Main Street and I was so tempted to stop a rickshaw and go to see them, but I could not venture out on my own. Picture me before the operation, with a sling bag on my shoulder, strutting off twice a week for meetings. Now, I had to wait for one of my children to hold my hand and take me for a walk just down the road as I dragged my foot painfully along. I could not walk on my own.

I know through all this, the Lord had a plan and purpose for my life. He was changing me to what He wants me to be. He was putting me through a fiery furnace, so that I could come out more precious than gold. He was 'crushing' me so that His 'fragrance' could penetrate through me. Every test and trial I went through was only to strengthen and purify me.

It is so wonderful to know that He is not working in me alone. Our Lord, the Master Craftsman, is busy shaping and moulding each of His 'lively stones' to form part of His Church on earth. What are all our troubles on this earth in comparison with the perfect joy we will share with Him for all eternity?

CHAPTER 36

I had become quite used to being completely house-bound now, except for short walks down the road with help. Going to church was out of the question. I praise God for the Cassidys, who shared their cassettes with me. I listened to meaningful church services from The First Church of the Nazarene at Pasadena, California. These cassettes were a great blessing and encouragement to me. On Sunday evenings I was further blessed with the 'Fellowship Meetings' held at home. On Tuesdays, we had Bible Studies and Breaking of Bread. Unable to go to church, the church would come to me at home.

As the days and weeks passed, there seemed to be an improvement, though I still had pain off and on. I was back to teaching in "Happy Hours." However, I had someone to help me. Maria Rebello, who offered her services, was a real boon.

I even started cooking and baking. However, I had to be careful not to carry heavy things or to bend. If I dropped anything, I would try to pick it up with my toes. I became a regular 'toe-catcher.' Since I was unable to retrieve some articles I would leave these telltale signs after me in all the rooms. Someone had to follow me and do the needful.

My children were anxious that I should get a second opinion before I ventured going outdoors again. I kept delaying for some reason or the other. A friend took my X-rays to a leading orthopedic surgeon. After looking at them he said I needed a very major operation, but nobody would take the risk of doing such an operation in India. Naturally, I fought shy of going to doctors. I accepted the fact that I would have to spend the rest of my life in pain, and yet I still did not pray for healing at this time, believing this was the Father's will for me.

Our Father's timing, however, is so perfect. How much He cares for His children, even more than He cares for the little sparrow that falls to the ground. In August 1985, Maria spoke to a doctor who was willing to come home and examine me. It is unusual for a civilian doctor to go out of his way to examine a patient at home without charging a fee. I can only say that this was God's infinite plan and perfect time. Dr. Sharad Chaudhari came home and examined me on that memorable day in August 1985.

After seeing my X-rays he was absolutely frank with me. He told me I would have to be operated again and soon. It was most essential. I asked if I could wait till December. I wanted to wait for Robin's vacation. Dr.Chaudhari said, "No! It must be done soon and very soon." He made the operation sound so simple. "I will just take eight inches of bone from your leg and divide it into two. Then I will fix these two grafts onto your spine. Soon you will be up and about and normal once again." It sounded as simple as an Art and Craft lesson in "Happy Hours."

He had so much confidence in himself and what is more, he instilled that same confidence in me as well. I agreed with everything he said by shaking my head vigorously and decided to have the operation. It was only after he left that the truth really dawned on me. I grabbed Patty who was at home that morning and cried my eyes out. I was scared! Some months earlier, I had said that I never wanted to have another operation in my life. And here, I agreed to have one done in less than a year. Dr. Chaudhari said that one jerk could cause me to be a paraplegic for life.

It was this that made me decide to go through the pain and discomfort of a second operation. I did not want to be a burden to my children or anyone else for the rest of my days. There was so much to pray about. I had to prepare myself physically, emotionally, mentally, spiritually and financially.

A heavy cloud hovered over '79' once again. How could we break this news to Robin now? And yet, I could not possibly hide it from him. What could I say without alarming him? It was too much of a shock for us at home. But we had each other to comfort and console. What about him? I wrote to him, but knowing how long letters take to reach, I decided to phone him after I received the results of my latest X-rays.

I phoned Mitzi in Calcutta to inform her of the latest developments. Since she had some leave to her credit, she came as soon as possible realizing the seriousness of the operation.

I had to reach out to God's Word continuously to gain more strength and confidence. I opened to Deuteronomy 3: 24 where I had underlined this verse earlier. Now it had new meaning for me. *"O Sovereign Lord, You have begun to show your servant Your greatness and Your strong hand. For what god is there in heaven or on earth who can do the deeds and mighty works You do?"* I looked further down to Chapter 4: 7 *"What other nation is so great as to have their gods near them the way the Lord our God is near us whenever we pray to Him?"* I derived much strength from these reassuring verses.

I would wake in the early hours of the morning and talk with the Lord. I would ask His guidance in big and in small matters. This time there was no waiting for miraculous gifts. He made it clear that I would have to humble myself and ask my family members for help and this is what I did. A couple of them came forward and helped me initially and later, many who belonged to the Family of God were most generous again.

We decided that Robin should not come home this time. We did not want him to miss another term. Each time I phoned him or he phoned, I was as brave as could be. As soon as the phone was down, I would cry my heart out longing for him to be home. But the Lord was teaching me to be dependant on Him alone.

Some of my friends did not like the idea of me having the operation. But it was clear in my mind that I should go ahead with it. Here again, God spoke to me through His Word from the book of Isaiah 30: 20-21. *The Lord will make you go through hard times, but He Himself will be there to teach you, and you will not have to search for Him anymore. If you wander off the road to the right or the left, you will hear His voice behind you saying, "Here is the road. Follow it." (GNB)*

It was clear that the road I had to follow was to the Poona Hospital to have this operation. I was admitted in this hospital on the ninth September and was operated three days later.

Talk of pain. It was unbearable! At least, I had the guarantee I was not going through it alone. While I went through all that pain, I was able to say, "My Lord, if I think this is bad, I am sure it is nothing compared to what You underwent for my sins and the sins of the world."

The Lord provided comfort in my daughters, Cheryl and Patty. They cared for me in such an expert way and showered me with love. Even the doctor remarked on their capability. Since the hospital was short-staffed, he allowed me to go home sooner than usual, knowing I would be well cared for at home. I was virtually invalid. Overnight, my girls had a load of responsibilities on their shoulders. They had to see to my Nursery, the cooking, the house, and took turns to nurse me.

I must say they made excellent nurses and house-keepers. I can never ever thank God enough for all they did for me; they undertook the most menial tasks even, so lovingly. The Lord surely gave them the strength and the ability to face each day's tasks with a smile and never complain at all.

I have so much to praise and thank God for. Today the pain and discomfort is all in the past. There is a vast improvement; I am able to accomplish so very much, but I have to know when to stop and put on the brakes.

CHAPTER 37

W hat has the Lord meant in all this to me? There is one thing I am glad about. Since I was unable to complete this book after the first operation, the Lord gave me time with a second operation to do so. Again my question to the Lord is, "What will You have me do Lord?" I wait for His command and I will obey. Whatever happens in our lives happens according to His plan. *"And we know that in all things God works for the good of those who love Him, who have been called according to His purpose."* (Romans 8: 28)

When I review my life, I see how the Lord saved me for a specific purpose. He saved me from those three accidents in 1969. He saved me from two major operations. Over and above, He has saved me for all eternity. He has saved me and given me eternal life because of my belief and trust in Jesus Christ as my Lord and Savior.

I wanted children. He gave them to me...three precious children. He saved me all those years to take care of them and bring them up in the knowledge and fear of the Lord. It was an added blessing that my children and I grew together spiritually. We were bound with cords of love that could never be broken. We were so united to one another and to God. People admired our family for its closeness and its unity.

Christ was the very center of our lives and our home. We knew we could never face a single day on our own. In all things, big and small, we approached our Father's throne. He always guided us in all the decisions we had to take.

It was in February 1986,as I lay in bed resting after school, that Ruthie Gilbert, our dear friend who lived down the road, dropped in to see me. Both Ruthie and her husband Rod were working with Scripture Union in Maharashtra.

After breezing in from the back door, as was customary with all our friends, Ruthie entered my bedroom with a wide smile and seated herself on my bed. After a few preliminaries, she asked me what I would be like after three months.

"Three months?" I replied, "I do not know what I will be like tomorrow Ruth, and here you ask me about three months!"

Quick thoughts flashed through my mind. 'What is Ruth after? Does she want me to speak at the next S.U. Camp? Does she want me to take care of Ben her second son, while she and little Danny go to England?' She went on asking me and honestly I was quite foxed. Then she could contain herself no longer and said that her parents, Maureen and George Swannell, wanted to send a ticket for me to accompany her to England for a holiday in May.

I was dumbfounded. I did not even possess a passport. How would I manage? I was unable to walk with confidence on my own. I still dragged my left foot and needed someone to hold onto for support. I reminded Ruthie of all my physical disabilities and asked her how would I manage. "Have no fear," she said, "We will get you a wheel chair at the airport."

When it suddenly dawned on me what was going to happen, I let out a loud Red Indian war cry! I was so excited. I told Ruthie everything seemed to be against me, but if this was God's will He would work out every detail for me. It was then that I recalled a prophecy I had received in 1977 at a Convention at New Life Center. The speaker had asked if any of us needed prayers for healing. If not for ourselves, we could go up on behalf of anyone else. I decided to go and pray for my mum's eyesight, which she nearly lost while expecting me. As I stood there with head bowed and downcast eyes, the speaker came around laying hands and praying for each individual's needs. When she approached me I waited for her to pray healing prayers. Instead I heard her say, "Behold I have chosen you to be My handmaiden to spread my message to all nations."

My face was burning and my heart skipped a few beats! She walked ahead and I was about to return to my place when she came back with oil and anointed me. "Be humble handmaiden, it will not be you speaking but I will speak through you," I then heard her say. I returned to my place deliriously happy and blessed at having been chosen by the Lord. I kept these words hidden in my heart. Now nine years later,

I was offered a trip to England. Perhaps this was how the Lord was going to fulfill this prophecy!

Being unable to travel in a rickshaw, I could not venture to Main Street, to have my passport photograph taken. We found an old snap and had Milton, the photographer from Main Street do the needful. Passport forms were duly filled and signed from my bed, and sent to Bombay. In record time, every detail was seen to and on 8th May 1986, I flew to England by British Airways with Ruthie, Ben and little Danny. I was quite nervous at first, being my maiden flight, but later, I felt like a real veteran and enjoyed the flight and all the service on board the aircraft.

Maureen and George Swannell were at Heathrow Airport to welcome us. They were so kind and warm and loving. I could not imagine how they could spend such an exorbitant sum of money for my ticket. These dear friends preferred investing their money on people rather than on **things**. I enjoyed every moment of my stay in England. God used me to share my testimony in a number of Fellowship groups.

From England, He planned that I should visit Scotland for a week. This time, He used Lily Murphy as His instrument. She kindly paid my fare to Scotland. I had first met Lily when she was visiting India and had attended one of the fellowship meetings at our home. Lily was a gracious hostess and showed me as much as we could manage in my short stay. I also visited all the friends I knew from India including my dear friends Sheila and John Mc Leod. I spent a few days with them and was amazed to see

Rory and Hamish. I just could not picture them as my Nursery school children! They towered above me!

When I returned from Scotland, there was a letter from Cedric, my brother in law inviting me to New York! Was this true? I, who had never sat in an aeroplane before, was now flitting from one end of the world to the other, all in the space of a month! I realized that health is not the criteria, neither is finance. God is able to do **ALL** things and much more than we dare to dream of or ask Him. He used me for His glory as I shared my testimony of what He had done in my life, wherever I went. I recalled Psalm 118, which I had read before my first operation; *"I will not die, but live, and will proclaim what the Lord has done."*

When I returned to England from New York, I found there was a delay in our return to India, as little Danny was sick and admitted in hospital. I had some bonus time thrown in. During this period I heard there was a 'Praise and Worship' evening where different churches were meeting together. On this particular evening, I was in excruciating pain. The dragging of my foot was more pronounced.

Ruthie's sister in law Joy drove me to this meeting. She helped me into the church and we sat on the last bench, so that I could rest my head against the wall. There was a dynamic speaker who delivered the message. After the message, he asked if people needed prayers for healing. He listed a number of ailments people might be suffering from. Suddenly he said, "There is someone here with a severe backache." My ears immediately pricked up. Then he told us to remain in our places and lay our hand on that particular part of the body while he prayed for us.

While he prayed, I felt something go through my body. I took a few steps out of my place and as I did so, I realized I could walk without dragging my foot. I was overjoyed as I thanked and praised the Lord for His healing power that was going through me.

The preacher then asked if anyone needed special prayers to come forward. Both Joy and I watched amazed as one after the other who had gone forth were being 'slain in the Spirit.' Both of us started discussing what we observed. Joy wanted prayer but did not want to fall down. So she told me she would go and plant her feet firmly on the ground. I said I could not afford to be dropped down with the condition of my back.

Joy walked up and I stood where I could see her. But where was she? I looked all over! Joy was slain in the Spirit and was on the ground with the others. I dared to walk forward and told one of the Elders that I desired prayers. I explained my back problem and my fear of falling. So they kindly got me a chair and I was told to sit with my legs stretched forward. The Minister touched my feet lightly and prayed. I felt my legs tingling and moving about. I was crying with happiness. I walked out of church without holding onto Joy. All the way home we sang praises to our loving and miracle working God. We were so grateful that we could be present at this wonderful Praise and Healing meeting, and experience a touch from the Lord.

"He's able, He's able,

I know He's able.
I know my Lord is able,
To carry me through.
He heals the broken hearted
And sets the captives free
He makes the lame to walk again
And makes the blind to see."

Yes, my God is able to heal. I definitely felt His touch that day. But two days later, as I was packing to return to India, I strained my back and had much pain after standing for a length of time.

I returned to Poona with pleasant memories of my trip abroad and a grateful heart to all the dear people who made this trip possible. I thanked my loving God and Father for giving me this wonderful opportunity, for I know without Him, it would not have been possible.

CHAPTER 38

Back again I came to "Happy Hours" and my Nursery children. A few months later, the pain in my back and leg grew worse. X-rays and more X-rays were taken. The results were not good.

In September 1987, I was led to a sports doctor, who advised me to join a Health Gym in the city. He said daily exercise would be most beneficial. I went there faithfully for a couple of months, but it was getting too expensive and too tiring for me to go there daily after school. Surely, there was an easier solution.

On making enquiries, I found there was someone who could fabricate the equipment I required. Soon I had my own gym; I was able to exercise daily at home. This helped me tremendously. I found I could now walk much better. I stopped limping and dragging my foot. What a difference the exercise made to my life. I had less pain and more freedom. I was ready to go places once again! Surely the Lord was preparing me for what was ahead. Almost out of the blue, I received an invitation to attend the June 1989

Advanced Leadership Training at the Haggai Institute in Singapore. This is for women from Third World countries. It was such a blessing to meet with fellow believers from different walks of life. We were part of Dr. John Haggai's vision, to be trained in order to train other nationals on returning to our respective countries. This undoubtedly was a great challenge.

Come September 1989, I felt a jabbing pain in my back and a burning sensation down my left leg. It alarmed me. Yet more X-rays were called for. The verdict: a third operation! A bigger, more delicate operation was essential with chances of success that would make a card sharp sweat. Success could mean a corrected spine; failure could mean paralysis. I would have to lose weight! Again, the seriousness of it was spelled out.

I started the campaign to lose weight in earnest. Those X-rays were shown to doctors in Poona, Bangalore, Vellore and Singapore. Everywhere the verdict was the same. I must have the operation, or else! This time, however, I prayed for healing. I asked the Lord to rule out the operation. I believed that whatsoever I asked in faith, I would receive.

Years have gone by and Praise God I have not been operated neither have I become paralyzed! I rush about in rickshaws on roads full of potholes. My back gets jerked about as I travel on the roads, and yet...no operation! I do not need support to walk. I do not drag my foot any longer. At times, however, I do get reminders and then I realize I must take precautions and be careful. Anyone seeing me go about will never believe that the X-rays belong to me. God is great! He is wonderful! Praise His Holy Name. I am a 'walking miracle.'

During my time of anxiety in September 1990, I was invited to Singapore again. But this time I was asked to be the Resident Coordinator at the Haggai Institute. Despite the possibility of yet another operation, or that of becoming paralyzed, I took this step in faith and was able to perform all the duties extremely well with the Lord's grace and strength.

I found again and again, that I could do even the impossible when I put my trust in Him. I love my Lord and I know He loves me dearly and unconditionally. I want to continue to serve the Lord with all my heart. I know His will for me is to share His love with others. Because of this, I used to conduct Bible Studies at the Nursing Cadets' Mess in Poona. It was a blessing to go and share God's Word with these hungry souls. What joy it was to see these girls grow and mature in the Lord.

My desire in life, is to fulfill the Lord's Great Commission in Matthew 28:18 - 20 where His last words to His disciples were *"All authority in heaven and on earth has been given to Me. Therefore go and make disciples of all nations, baptizing them in the name of the Father, and of the Son, and of the Holy Spirit, and teaching them to obey everything I have commanded you. And surely I am with you always, to the very end of the age."*

My X-rays show one thing, but I have no pain and discomfort like before. God has certainly healed me in His own way. I truly believe I can do all things through Christ who strengthens me. I can say, there is no fear of an operation, no need of fearing about tomorrow. I am healed today. And today, I will do whatever the Lord wants me to do and go wherever He commands me to go. Tomorrow is another day!

I have not take any painkillers for a long time. I have dared to climb up to the third floor without a complaint, whereas I could not even manage a single step formerly! Not only have I received physical healing but also spiritual healing. Barriers are being pulled down. Christ is using me to let His love shine through the neighborhood and elsewhere.

My Lord has taught me some wonderful lessons through pain and suffering. It has all been in His mighty plan. Every test and trial that comes our way is only to strengthen us and purify us and make us even more precious than gold. These verses from the Bible are a constant encouragement to me. *"We are pressed on every side by trouble, but not crushed and broken. We are perplexed because we don't know why things happen as they do, but we don't give up and quit. We are hunted down but God never abandons us. We get knocked down but we get up again and keep going. These bodies of ours are constantly facing death just as Jesus did. So it is clear to us that it is only the living Christ within us who keeps us safe."* (2 Corinthians 4: 8-10 TLB)

"Though our bodies are dying, our inner strength in the Lord is growing every day. These troubles and sufferings of ours are, after all quite small and won't last very long. Yet this short time of distress will result in God's richest blessing on us forever and ever! So we do not look at what we can see right now,

the troubles all around us, but we look forward to the joys in heaven which we have not yet seen. The troubles will soon be over, but the joys to come will last forever." (2 Corinthians 4: 16 - 18)

When I look back over my life, I thank my Father God for the crushing which He has taken me through. It has surely brought out His fragrance in my life. I have experienced His love in more ways than one.

Prophet Isaiah says in chapter 40: 29-31 *"He gives power to the tired and worn out, and strength to the weak. Even the youths shall be exhausted and the young men will all give up. But they that wait on the Lord shall renew their strength. They shall mount up with wings like eagles; they shall run and not be weary; they shall walk and not faint."*

Yes, God has strengthened me and enabled me to do things far beyond my capability and imagination. No matter what I may face tomorrow, I will always praise and glorify my Lord Jesus Christ, for He is worthy to be praised.

CHAPTER 39

"There is a right time for everything. A time to be born; A time to die; A time to plant; A time to harvest; A time to kill; A time to destroy; A time to rebuild; A time to cry; A time to laugh; A time to grieve; A time to dance." **Ecclesiastes 3: 1-4**

Yes! There is a time for everything. Soon it was time for my children to find the love of their lives and settle down. One after the other the birds flew from their nest.

Cheryl married Peter in December 1986 and moved to Bangalore.

In November 1989 Patty married Henry and set off for Bombay.

Five months later, in April 1990, Robin left for Singapore to marry Lucy, his colleague from Singapore Bible College.

I was now all alone. I could literally 'hear' the silence. It was eerie at times. It was not at all easy. I questioned as to WHY we were such a close-knit family. It made the parting even more difficult to bear. When I saw other families meeting together for birthdays and other occasions, I would miss my family all the more.

What made matters worse was, that there were burglaries in the neighborhood nearly every night. These guys would prowl around at night with cloth steeped in chloroform and throw it into the house of their choice. Once they were certain the inmates were fast asleep, they would cut the grills and enter from the windows. By gaining entrance into the houses in this manner, they helped themselves to whatever they desired and then left with their loot.

When I heard these gruesome tales, I was petrified and wondered when they would visit me. I could not sleep for fear. I lay awake night after night and heard each hour chime through the stillness of the night. Yes! I trusted God and prayed for safety. Often I would say "I trust You Lord.... but!!" I am sure God wondered why I had to add the **buts;** instead I should have said, "I trust You Lord" and full stop.

As always God spoke to me from His Word. I was led to read Psalm 4: 8 which says, " *I will lie down in peace and sleep, for though I am alone O Lord, You will keep me safe"* I read and re-read this verse and clung to the promise, and believe you me that was the end of my fearful and sleepless nights. As soon as my head touched the pillow, I would drop into such a sound and peaceful sleep. I know my God

was taking care and watching over me. Psalm 121:
3 says *"He who keeps Israel neither slumbers nor
sleeps."* I believe He set His angels round my house
with flaming swords to keep at bay any undesired
person who passed by at night or day. We lived in that
house in St.Patrick's Town Poona for nearly thirty
years and there was not a single robbery or break - in
all that time. Praise His wonderful Name.

Now I looked forward to the holidays with more
excitement than my "Happy Hours" children did.
All my holidays were spent visiting my loved ones
who I missed so much. Each holiday was so special.
But getting back was the hardest part. It made the
loneliness even more unbearable. Was my life now
to be a series of periodic memorable reunions and
increasingly painful partings? Were love and the joys
of my grandchildren meant to be dispensed to my
aching soul like carefully measured wartime rations?
Everything that had become my world since Percy
died was now gone. What did God have in store for
me now?

It was in 1991, after spending a holiday with
Cheryl and Peter that I was returning to Poona, when
Peter suddenly came out with an offer that got me
thinking. I hadn't said a word to them and so it took
me by surprise. I remember clearly we were having
lunch at Chungwa, a Chinese Restaurant, when he
looked at me and said "Mum, you have worked so
hard and for so long, why don't you stop working
now and come and make your home with us? You
can use our home as a base and from here visit Robin
and Patty and who knows where else the Lord will

take you, now that your book is going to be released shortly?" Was he a prophet? Needless to say, I was speechless and had a lump in my throat as in a short time after we returned home; I would be leaving for the airport to return to Poona.

I asked Peter why didn't he discuss this at home the previous night, as I was so choked and unable to respond to him in the restaurant. I knew if I spoke I might start bawling there. When we went home and as I was doing my last minute packing, I asked him what should I do with my Nursery. To which he replied, "Close it." Easier said than done! All the way to Poona I prayed and asked the Lord to show me His will. I did not want to do anything out of His will.

The very next morning I started getting admissions for the new school year and instead of being excited over them, I asked the parents to wait for some time, as I was not taking any new admissions right away. But then, something had to be done with the pupils who were already with me. I didn't have the guts to face the parents, so after a few days I wrote a note asking them to make arrangements for admissions for their children in other schools for the New Year. I duly pinned these notes on the children and sent them home. Oh what a volley of questions I had to face the following day when the parents came to confront me, but I seemed to manage it quite well.

You would think with the loving letters and calls I had received from Bangalore, I should have been rejoicing and excited, but no! I felt myself tossing about at night and sometimes even crying wondering about my future. Why did I feel like this? I shared this with my pastor and asked him to pray for me. Patty happened to come home for a weekend from Bombay and I shared my fears with her. We prayed and asked for God's guidance. Now I was jobless, as I had told the parents to get admissions for their children in other schools.

Neelu -- one of the parents who was helping in my Nursery and Patty asked if I really wanted to close the Nursery. Perhaps I didn't want to, but having that wonderful invitation of staying with my children, made me think that this is what I should do. So now I decided to carry on with the Nursery for some time. I called Cheryl and Peter and mentioned my decision. I wrote notes again to the parents stating that school would close in April and reopen in June and if anyone was desirous of sending their children back to "Happy Hours" to inform me. I felt such a fickle person! Again I didn't have the guts to face the parents eyeball to eyeball, so the notes were pinned onto the children.

The next morning I was confronted by the parents who came with the notes I had written and said, "You said you were closing the Nursery," to which I replied, "Yes..."

"Now you say you are reopening it." And sheepishly I replied, "Yes."

"Are **you** going to run it?"

"Yes I am."

"Are you sure that **you** are going to run it?"

I had to reassure them that I would be running the Nursery. And then...what did I hear most of them say? "If you are going to run it, we will bring our children back." They had already paid their admission fees for the following year and some had even paid three months fees, but having my word that I would continue, all of them except two parents readmitted their children. This was a real confirmation that this is where the Lord wanted me to be. How grateful I was to God and to the parents, and to Patty and Neelu.

Relieved that this ordeal was settled, I went to spend a part of my summer holiday with Patty and Henry and their boys in Bombay and then onto Bangalore to Cheryl, Peter and their girls. Robin, who had come from Singapore for some time, accompanied me. Suddenly one night when I had gone to the toilet I found myself in excruciating pain in my back. I could not move, nor could I take a step. I cried out to Robin to come and give me a hand. He had to carry me to my bed and I was in agony for the rest of the night. I thought I was going to get paralyzed. Then came all the questions to God. "If You knew this was going to happen to me, why did You let me reopen my Nursery? Why did You let me tell the parents that I would be running it?" I was desperate. Robin decided he would go back to Poona and ask Neelu to run it for me. "Oh what will the parents say?" I prayed so much but nothing could be done. The pain was terrible and unbearable.

Dr. Benjamin Isaac came over to examine me the next morning and said I had an inflammation on the spine, which caused the pain. I had to have complete bed rest and heavy painkillers. When the inflammation improved he said that he would give me acupressure. Praise the Lord with all the treatment I had, I was healed and was able to go back and run my Nursery in Poona.

I had wondered why I had felt the way I did, about re-locating to Bangalore, especially since Cheryl and Peter had given me such a warm and loving welcome. We see the here and now but God sees our yesterdays, our todays and tomorrows at a glance. A few months later Peter's parents suddenly decided to leave Bombay and settle in Bangalore in the same place where I had been invited to stay. Can you imagine if I had accepted Cheryl and Peter's invitation? I would have rented my house in Poona and come to Bangalore with my bag and baggage. I dread to think what would have happened! The Lord knows best and when we commit our ways into His hands, He will lead and direct us all the way. Thank You Lord.

And so "Happy Hours" continued in full swing and it did so till 1995 after I ran it for twenty-five years. The parents quietly planned a function to mark this special occasion. I was touched. Not only did we celebrate the silver jubilee of "Happy Hours" but now it was definitely farewell also. I received a phone call from Cheryl informing me that two flats were going for sale in the same apartment in Bangalore and suggested that I should come to the flat on the first floor and they would take the one on the third floor. I was so excited and at peace. I knew it was God's perfect time and plan for me. Everything worked out so quickly. Within the week I had a buyer for my house and I handed over the extra Nursery children to Rashida who was helping me in "Happy Hours." The parents knew her and hence willingly sent their children to the Nursery she was opening close by.

In September 1995, it was goodbye to "Happy Hours" and to my home, which I had seen come up brick by brick. I left Poona full of peace and joy into the unknown. I had no idea what I was going to do, taking early retirement, but God knew. In fact He has planned things for each of us even before Creation. It was great coming to Bangalore so close to my daughters and their families, as Patty and Henry were also transferred here. Once I surrendered my life and my all to Jesus and depended on Him entirely, He worked it out that we could be together again.

I was so content to be close to my family. I was 'retired' and satisfied. But does a child of God ever retire from the plan of the Father? Certainly not! God had plans for me. I thought that going to Bangalore was an end in itself; but to God it was merely a threshold into a new phase of His promise for my life.

CHAPTER 40

There was a writer's and publisher's conference in Feb.1996 and I was invited to attend with the hope of meeting a publisher to reprint my book. I went along and approached various publishers but did not seem to be too successful. One day while I was pouring over the manuscript, I found some pages missing, and wondered what should be done about it, when Peter approached me and told me that I should become the publisher. "You must be kidding," said I. "First the Lord tells me to be a writer, now you want me to be a publisher. How does one do that?"

Well we found out that all that one needs is a name, a rubber stamp and a bank account. Ha ha!!! Any fool can be a publisher! So we thought of a name. He suggested a few. Then I had a brainwave. "Since I am a Newnes why don't we call it The Newness Of Life Publications" and I sketched an appropriate logo. From wanting to become a nun, I became a Newnes and now overnight... the proprietress of Newness of Life Publications!

Good! Yippee; now I am a publisher!! But do you think that was enough for Peter Hendricks? No way! He then persuaded me to buy a computer. "Whatever for?" I asked. "I don't even know how to type." And this son-in-law of mine says "Learn. It's never too late to do so." Between him and Henry they got me to buy a computer and had it set up for the new up and coming publisher! He even bought me a book for Dummies!! Quite an impression of his ma - in - law!

Well this retired teacher was sure a 'dummy' when it came to the computer. So often I would call either Peter or Henry when I was stuck and ask them what I was supposed to do. There were times I would even call Robin in Singapore to help me with my problems!

They were willing to teach me and help me. Till late at night I would sit and key in the book, wrong fingering and all complete. All went well till a little box would appear with a question and for the love of me, I did not know what to answer, and swish… six chapters of my effort were wiped out in the twinkling of an eye. This happened twice. Then I seemed to get the hang of it and had completed twenty chapters. There came the question again! Ask me today what the question was and I still don't know! Believe it or not, I did "tick tack too here I go, If I miss I'll take this"…. and blindly pointed the mouse and clicked and with that twenty chapters disappeared.

I left my seat and said "Lord, I am not going to cry, but I would like to know what You are teaching me through all this?" And then I was told I should commit it to Him. Glory!! Who else was it committed to? The whole idea of the book was His! "It's Yours Lord." And then like an inner voice said to me, "**Every** time you sit at the computer commit it to Me." The Lord is such a loving and gentle teacher. This made me realize we can be saved ages ago, baptized in the Holy Spirit years ago but what are we like today? What we need to have is a daily commitment, nay a moment-to-moment dedication of our lives to Jesus. The lessons came through loud and clear and praise the Lord I completed the book without knowing anything about the computer. Let me tell you, I still don't know much at all, but I press on regardless.

Operation Mobilization Secunderabad did the finishing touches to the book and the second edition was ready by 1996. So now from Principal of "Happy Hours" I became Publisher of Newness of Life Publications and was kept as busy as ever.

From a year as wandering Jew (shuffling to and fro from one child's home to the other) I had reached Bangalore and the Promised Land of publishing. It flowed with the milk of new technology and the honey of family togetherness. I didn't need to visit Jerusalem. Or maybe I did!

Before the thought could even cross my mind, my cousin Marina an air hostess dropped in. "Oh guess what? I am off to the Holy Land in April 1997" she casually said over lunch. Jokingly I asked her if she needed someone to carry her bags. She thought I was so keen to go, that she informed the leader of the tour group about me. And soon I found that I was involved in getting ready to join the party. Marina suddenly was informed she could not make this trip so here was I going alone with people I didn't know at all. How would I manage? But once we met, we got to know each other and were very excited.

Sad to say, the visit was only for a week. Much too short to take in everything there is to offer. But oh! What an experience. It was a chance of a lifetime. The Bible became so real to me. I could picture things and places in such a realistic way after that memorable trip. It was a privilege and honor being chosen to go to the Holy Land. We had an excellent guide Helen, who brought to life the stories of the Bible. As we sailed on the Lake of Galilee she pointed to us 'the city that never can be hidden.' At the distance we spotted Capernaum where Jesus met Peter, Andrew, James and John and told them to follow Him.

We sauntered by the ruins of Peter's house, stood on the spot where Jesus fed the five thousand men with five loaves of bread and two fish. We prayed at Gethsemane, walked the route of the Via Dolorosa. It was so interesting to see ruins of old Roman cities, which had been excavated in the past thirty to forty years. It was a blessing to see where Jesus was born, grew up and then died. It was so awesome because we know one day soon Jesus will return descending from the skies to the new Jerusalem. His feet will rest once again on Mt.Olives, as He will receive all those who trust Him as their Lord and Savior. We celebrated our Sunday service at the Garden Tomb that was something I can never forget. All too soon the week came to an end, but those memories will linger till I go back there again to meet Jesus.

The week flew and I returned to my emotional Jerusalem. Life was busy. There was family and friends and a full program at Full Gospel Assembly of God Church where we had become members. Life had settled...but not for long.

In 1998 my feet started itching and I thought of the prophecy I had in 1977. Where should I go? What about Australia? I decided to drop in at Singapore on my way there and back to visit Robin, Lucy and Nicky as I was allowed three free stops on my ticket. I chose Brisbane, Sydney and Melbourne. Once I was there, two friends of mine, paid for me to also visit Adelaide, Perth and New Zealand. When I was purchasing my ticket I knew I would have to break my fixed deposit and I said, "Lord if I go on doing this what will I have to live on?" And immediately came the reply "What did you live on in the past? Who took care of you in the past?" I had to say "Sorry Lord" and I went ahead.

God wants us to trust Him completely and depend on Him alone. All I had to do was touch the river Jordan with the tip of my foot in faith and then He made a way for me. Churches just opened their doors for me to share my testimony nearly every Sunday and also during the week. It was great witnessing what the Lord had done in my life. As I shared my testimony, people wanted to purchase a copy of my book.

A few years later, as I was watching a TV program one night, the preacher said, "Nothing is impossible with God." I stretched my hand to the TV and prayed, "Lord, I know nothing is impossible with You. If

You want me to go on another trip will You give me money without me getting help from anyone for it?" Two days later, I received a letter from the Bank asking me to come and sign some forms, which I had applied for **two years previously.** Nothing happens by coincidence! I asked the Lord and He worked immediately. These forms had something to do with Percy's back pension, which was due to me. What a great God we have. His timing is absolutely perfect.

Before this happened Patty came over one morning and asked me what I was doing about my trip and I promptly said "Praying." But she -- the practical one said that I had to do something as well. So I decided to call the agent and told her the places I would like to visit. When she asked me what was my budget I said "Nothing." She must have thought I was bonkers. I told her once I knew the cost I would pray about it and God would give it to me and give it He did.

So off I went to Dubai, England, Scotland, Ireland, and Switzerland and back to Dubai. What a fruitful trip it was sharing my testimony wherever I went and taking "Crushed for Fragrance" with me. All these trips are in fulfillment of the prophecy I had in 1977 that God would use me among the nations. I knew it was God speaking through me wherever I went, as He had promised.

Whilst in England, I had lunch with Monika, a flight attendant of United Airlines. I presented her with my book. She was touched after reading it. Before I left England she came to visit me and asked me when would I come on my next trip to Europe? I told her it depended on the Lord. "Then what about England?" she asked. I said that too depended on the Lord as I got my orders from Him. "Well," she continued "if you can make a trip to Delhi next April, perhaps I can get you a ticket from there to England and then take you on to Germany to visit my mother, who I am sure you would be able to speak to and encourage as she had cancer and is very bitter with life." I wondered who I would stay with in Delhi, but left it at that!

There was no further news from Monika but lo and behold! Henry got a new job and was posted to Gurgaon just twenty minutes away from the airport in Delhi. "Lord what are You trying to tell me?" Henry and Patty invited me to their home in January 2001 to be with them, Shaphan and Ruel. I stayed with them for nearly two months. Whilst there, I emailed Monika and asked if the invitation was still open to which she replied in the affirmative. I returned to Bangalore for three weeks and had to collect some documents and my passport before returning to Delhi with Cheryl, Peter, Tammy and Jeanine. We had a wonderful family holiday together.

Since I was going to England, I decided I would break my fixed deposit and go to Canada to meet all my friends and relations there and to also meet an aunt who I came to know on the Internet. Her husband Stu, however, was most generous and said that he would pay for my ticket and stay there. So God had it all fixed for me this time. I went with Monika to Nurnberg where I enjoyed seeing this very pretty and historical place. Not knowing each other's language was a problem, so Monika had to be the interpreter as I spoke to her parents and shared the love of Jesus with them. Seeds were sown in their hearts and I can only pray for God's Spirit to work in their lives.

From Germany I spent a few days in England visiting friends before I left for Canada to be with aunt Ruby and Stu. They gave me a warm welcome and took good care of me. I met school friends and relations I hadn't met for thirty to forty years and had a wonderful time with them. I spread the love of Jesus wherever I went, sharing what He had done in my life.

The highlight of my trip was being invited to share my testimony live on the Crossroads TV program at 100 Huntley Street. I was thrilled and excited but nervous. I trusted Jesus and He saw me through. People were blessed. I ended the interview telling the listeners "Jesus is the **only** answer for the world today. No matter, what your problems are, cast your burdens upon Him for He cares for you. You are precious to Jesus and He loves you. He will turn your darkness into light, your sorrows into gladness. He will fill the empty vacuum in your life and give you a purpose for living. He did it for me when I was crushed and broken and He will surely do it for anyone else."

In 2004, I visited Canada again and once more was invited to Crossroads at 100 Huntley Street, for a morning programme and then for the night programme - Nite Lite from 2 a.m to 4.30 a.m. It was such an immense privilege and honor. I can say this is all because of what God has planned and ordained for me to be used as His humble handmaiden. Praise His wonderful name.

I still say that I have no idea what the morrow holds, but I know who holds the morrow in His hands. I don't know what Jesus has in store for me but I want to be available for His work wherever He leads me, to be used for His glory. I realize all God wants is our availability and He gives us the ability. Truly He chooses the simple ones of this world to be used for His glory. If we are faithful in small things He will entrust us with larger things. I, who would not dare speak in public before, can do all things through Christ who strengthens me.

God is still working in me. I am still weak and do fail many times but He is so loving and He is teaching me slowly but surely and is changing me. It is so thrilling, living each day for Him and depending on Him. The important thing I have learned is to surrender completely to Jesus. I have learned that whatever little is in my hand I must give it over to Him and see what He can do with it.

From 1996 I started a quarterly publication called 'The Fragrance' where people send in their testimonies exalting the Name of Jesus. I send this publication to many countries in the world to people who are on my mailing list. I have also started a web page at: --www.geocities.com/margaretnewnes where 'The Fragrance' is printed for many others to read. My aim is to let the "Fragrance of Jesus" be seen in and through my life and I would like His fragrance to spread all over the world.

WORD FROM THE
WRITER

Do you feel crushed, laden with sorrow, not knowing where to turn? I want you to know that you can turn to Jesus who was crushed for our iniquities. He is the answer, the only answer for your every problem...physical, spiritual, mental, material...in fact, just about any and every problem. There is no problem too big, which He cannot solve, and no problem too small, which He will not care about. We try to solve our problems on our own and get nowhere in the end.

Sometimes we go on as if this life is everything but we must remember, we are only pilgrims on this earth. One day we will all have to meet Jesus our Judge, no matter what religion or background we come from.

Jesus promised He would return to this earth one day. We do not know when that day will be. He will come like a thief in the night. If the owner of the house knew when the thief would come, he would stay ready and prepared but he does not know the time, so he has to be prepared always. Neither do we know when Jesus will return. We know He is coming, so we too must be ready and prepared always.

If you want to be ready to meet Jesus, do not wait for tomorrow. Tomorrow may never come. **Today** is the day of salvation. Today is the day to repent of your sins and confess them to Jesus. Only Jesus can offer you eternal life and salvation.

Remember, no religion can save you. Good works cannot gain you eternal life. All the degrees in the world will not help you; neither can you buy your way there. Why is it that we cannot earn our way to heaven? Because man is a sinner.

The Bible says in Romans 3: 23 *"For all have sinned and fall short of the glory of God."* We are all sinners before a holy and just God; the Bible makes it very clear.

As sinners, we have to pay the penalty of our sin. *"For the wages of sin is death..."* (Romans 6: 23).

There is no escape, but God in His infinite love for the world solved this problem in the person of Jesus Christ. *"For God so loved the world that He gave His only begotten Son that whosoever believes in Him shall not perish, but have everlasting life."* (John 3: 16). Jesus died for the sins of the whole world. We must believe that His Blood alone can cleanse us from all our sins. We must confess that Jesus is Lord and believe that God raised Him from the dead.

"If you confess with your own mouth, 'Jesus is Lord' and believe in your heart that God raised Him from the dead, you will be saved. For it is with your heart that you believe and are justified, and it is with your mouth that you confess and are saved." (Romans 10: 9-10).

Jesus is waiting for you to invite Him into your heart. *"Behold I stand at the door and knock. If anyone hears My voice and opens the door, I will come in and sup with him and he with Me."* (Revelation 3:20). You have to open the door from within and He will come in. Jesus will never force His way into your heart. You have to be willing; and once He enters, He will never leave you nor forsake you.

When you invite Jesus to be the Lord and Savior of your heart, you will be able to face any crushing in this life. You will not be facing it alone; He will always be there to help you. What is more, you will experience the fragrance of His love and grace spreading from your life and blessing others for His glory.

"For through what Christ has done, He has triumphed over us so that now wherever we go, He uses us to tell others about the Lord and to spread the gospel like a sweet perfume. As far as God is concerned there is a sweet, wholesome fragrance in our lives. It is the fragrance of Christ within us, an aroma

to both the saved and the unsaved all around us." (2 Corinthians 2: 14-15)

If you have been blessed by reading this book, please write to the address below:

Mrs. Margaret Newnes
103 Ave Maria Apts
25 Viviani Road
Richard's Town
Bangalore - 560 005
INDIA

Lightning Source UK Ltd.
Milton Keynes UK
UKHW040310061218
333518UK00001B/6/P

9 781604 774351